Best Practices in Adult Learning

A Self-Evaluation Workbook for Colleges and Universities

Thomas Flint

Paul Zakos

Ruth Frey

For the Council for Adult and Experiential Learning
(CAEL)

KENDALL/HUNT PUBLISHING COMPANY
4050 Westmark Drive   Dubuque, Iowa 52002

Table of Contents

Appendices

Foreword

By Morris T. Keeton

Senior Scholar, Institute on Research and Assessment in Higher Education, University of Maryland University College
President Emeritus, CAEL

This workbook continues a long and rich tradition of effort and innovation by CAEL (Council for Adult and Experiential Learning) and allied organizations to promote best practices beneficial to adult learners in higher education. An appreciation of this workbook must grow from the recognition of the many initiatives and influences that precede it.

The idea that adults should return to college for further education was not accepted in nineteenth century America, not even in the movement to establish land grant institutions (e.g., in the Morrill Act of the early 1960s and its later extension in the 1890s). Literacy education for adults (especially immigrants) was seen initially as a function of pre-collegiate schools or community agencies. At the turn of the 19th century, more than forty percent of American workers were in agriculture-related work that did not require postsecondary education. Four-year colleges and universities first began to give priority attention to adult students immediately after World War II, with the federal government's provision of veterans' education benefits and with President Truman's advocacy for two years of college to become a normal feature of citizens' lives. The veterans' response to these measures was the first large wave of adults to register for degree studies.

The impact of veterans on campus in the late 1940s was quite dramatic. They brought the wisdom of maturity and an element of seriousness about learning to the collegiate communities of the time. Appreciation for education's contribution to an overall quality of life seemed to take on a new weight because of the veterans' judgment about its importance to their own futures.

During World War II, the General Educational Development (GED) Examinations that assessed and recognized learning equivalent to that of high school completion were introduced. Shortly thereafter, in 1945, the American Council on Education (ACE) began to provide recommendations on recognition of service members' learning during their military service, thus facilitating awards of advanced standing and academic credit for many of them. With veterans, as contrasted with accomplished younger students, it was more evident to faculty that it was not sensible to require students to repeat learning that they had already mastered. The realization that the same policy might apply with other knowledgeable adults was not long in coming. In 1954, Brooklyn College introduced its "Special Baccalaureate Degree Program for Adults," which gave academic credit for learning derived from work and other experiences. By the early 1960s, in response to the need for less expensive education at the postsecondary level, the needs of increasing numbers of older adults, and the needs of students who wanted to attend part-time, the community college movement was well under way.

Also, a number of institutions began to offer degree programs designed especially for adults: the Bachelor of Liberal Studies at the University of Oklahoma (1961), the Goddard Adult Degree Program (1963), the Queens College Adult Continuing Education Program (1963), the Degree Completion Program at Mundelein (1965), the General Studies Program at Roosevelt University—which waived lower division work if students could complete upper division studies satisfactorily

(1966)—and University Without Walls programs in some twenty institutions and in eighteen Antioch College Centers by the late 1960s.

In the meantime, the sophistication of assessment practices was growing, as reflected by the introduction of the College Level Examination Program (CLEP) in 1967 by the College Entrance Examinations Board (CEEB, now College Board). In time, standardized instruments for both general education and for introductory-level disciplinary courses were developed.

Between 1968 and 1974, thirteen colleges were created with adult learners as the primary clientele and with some form of recognition of prior learning. The colleges included Empire State in New York, Metropolitan State in Minnesota, The College of Public and Community Service of University of Massachusetts-Boston, The Community College of Vermont, Thomas A. Edison State in New Jersey, The Regents College of the University of the State of New York, and Evergreen State of Washington. In Great Britain, the British Open University was established in 1971.

In her book, *Higher Education and the Real World: The Story of CAEL*, Zelda Gamson (1989) attributed the origin of CAEL to the convergence of this movement for non-traditional study, the development of the emerging adult education movement, and the growing sophistication in assessment.

From its very beginnings, CAEL has been determined to advocate for learner-friendliness on the part of colleges and universities—and even employers fostering employee development. The issue of "student-centeredness" surfaced at the initial meeting of the Steering Committee of the Cooperative Assessment of Experiential Learning (CAEL) Project at Educational Testing Service (ETS) in early March 1974. At that meeting, the concern was to find a way to assess what individuals had learned outside of formal schooling so that their claims to learning at the college or university level, rather than the unique coverage of particular courses at a given institution, could be the basis for judgment. Among other implications of that concern was the focus on individualized portfolios rather than standardized tests as a means of documenting the adults' achievements (Gamson, 1989).

A major development in CAEL's mission occurred in the late 1970s, when it became apparent that those who stood to benefit most from the recognition of extra-institutional learning by awards of academic credit or advanced standing were experienced adults. In 1977, when CAEL spun off from ETS management to become a free-standing association of colleges and universities, the meaning of its acronym was changed to "Council for the Advancement of Experiential Learning." The change meant that higher education itself should pay greater heed to broadening the experience base of its students (an achievement already common among mature adults) as well as to recognizing the knowledge and competence derived from such experiential learning (Gamson, 1989).

By the end of the 1970s, however, another name change had been adopted by the CAEL Trustees, to "Council for Adult and Experiential Learning." CAEL's endeavors in the late 1970s to influence colleges and universities to tailor their services toward the needs of adults had not met with much success, so a greater effort was mandated. Not only were universities of that period making minimal efforts to schedule classes at times and places convenient to working adults, but their admissions procedures in many instances still necessitated parental permission, such as parental agreement to guarantee tuition payments, and the like. If one were to ask a question such as why a university branch would subsidize Friday night dances but would not help with child care, the answer might be that while adults could go to dances, child care did not apply to all students, and that an institution should not provide services that did not benefit the student body as a whole.

In 1981, CAEL joined with the American Council on Education (ACE) in establishing its Commission on Higher Education and the Adult Learner. CAEL provided, through its Project LEARN, a partial match to ACE's support of the Commission, seconded the CAEL Executive to chair the Commission, and was active in all of its work. This Commission advocated with Congress and the Executive Branch of the U.S. Government for financial aid for part-time students, for removal or attenuation of the multitude of barriers (42 were cited) placed in the way of adults seeking to return to college (see Chapter 7 in *Employability in a High Performance Economy*), and enlisted the cooperation of the National Governors Association and the College Board in pressing for reforms (Sheckley, Lamdin, & Keeton, 1993).

Another key step in CAEL's leadership in promoting services to adult learners was taken in the fall of 1984. In that year, the UAW-Ford National Development and Training Center engaged Pamela Tate as its Senior Consultant for the development of its College and University Options Program. She, in turn, persuaded the Center to engage CAEL in the development of the Program and put it into operation in five states. This seminal development was the origin of what is now an array of employee growth and development programs based on partnerships between CAEL, employers, and, in cases of an organized workforce, labor unions. By 1999, these programs were serving more than 100,000 eligible workers throughout the United States.

Peter Smith, then Lieutenant Governor of the State of Vermont, devoted a chapter in his book *Your Hidden Credentials* (1986) to portraits of some adults who had benefited from the growing provisions for recognition of extra-collegiate learning. Foreshadowing a concept that CAEL was to more fully explore and promote in the late 1990s, Smith coined the term "Adult-Friendly College" to describe the new ways of thinking that had been promoted by the Commission on Higher Education and the Adult Learner, as well as the intended beneficiaries such as those served by CAEL's employee growth and development programs.

One of the projects of the ACE Commission was the development of a tool that institutions of higher education could use to assess their services to adult learners. With the help of grants from the Arthur Vining Davis Foundations and the Fund for the Improvement of Postsecondary Education, a guide for this activity was published and workshops were conducted across the country to assist institutions with identifying their strengths and weaknesses in serving adults and in selecting and undertaking improvements. This guide has now been revised and is again being used to assist in this type of improvement.

In light of the relatively large proportion of clients of alternative and external degree programs who were older adults, an association which is now called the Adult Higher Education Alliance (AHEA) developed and published, beginning in 1992, a statement of principles of good practice for such programs. These principles became a precursor of the CAEL-developed "Principles of Effectiveness" that form the framework of this workbook. The AHEA statement has been widely disseminated with the cooperation of ACE and CAEL. In 1995–1996, AHEA conducted, with the help of 20 colleges and universities, a Survey of Adult Learner Outcomes in which respondents were asked about the types of skills and knowledge they had achieved and about their relative importance. The AHEA also investigated the weighting given to different kinds of outcomes on the part of employers, students, and institutions of higher education.

Prior to the AHEA survey, in 1993, CAEL and ACE had carried out a collaborative study on quality assurance issues in degree programs for adults. The study included attention to abusive or incompetent practices in the awarding of credit for prior learning at colleges and universities, including so-called 'degree mills' (Stewart & Spille, 1988). A jointly sanctioned monograph on this matter was published and continues to be used ("Adult Degree Programs," 1993).

It was a natural next development that CAEL and the ACE, along with Regents College of New York and Empire State College, formed the Commission for a Nation of Lifelong Learners in 1996. The Commission was chaired by Morton Bahr, head of the Communications Workers of America, one of the largest organized labor unions in the United States, and led by a distinguished Board of corporate, governmental, labor, and higher education executives. In 1997, it held hearings across the U.S., co-hosted a conference with CAEL and the convening partners, and issued a final report. This event in turn set the stage for then Vice President Al Gore to convene a nationwide teleconference on Preparing the Workforce for Jobs of the Future, in 1999. The event involved one hundred downlinks throughout the country, featured best practice efforts in a number of diverse communities, and included announcement of new federal initiatives in support of education for the workforce. The effort may have played a role in the subsequent legislation (Section 127 of the IRS code) that permanently exempts tuition benefits paid by employers from being taxed as ordinary income to the employees.

CAEL has never confined its concerns or its efforts for student-centeredness to adults, but it has, as this series of events makes clear, been a devoted and determined advocate for adult learners. In the book *Employability in a High Performance Economy* (1993), the authors articulated a set of principles that characterize the best of employee development programs. These include:

- ❖ Giving the worker-learners choices in use of the benefits;
- ❖ Providing tools to help them make informed choices;
- ❖ Ensuring advocacy of the employability program by all partners;
- ❖ Providing access to the services for all employees, not just management;
- ❖ Engaging in proactive outreach to encourage participation;
- ❖ Providing prepaid tuition;
- ❖ Removing institutional barriers and disincentives among providers;
- ❖ Providing prior learning assessment;
- ❖ Providing workplace support systems, and
- ❖ Establishing and maintaining commitment to the values of adult learning.

Nor has CAEL's service to adult learners been confined to the United States as originally envisioned. During the 1980s, CAEL was invited by Norman Evans and the Learning From Experience Trust to assist in Great Britain's work in this cause. CAEL also responded to invitations from British Columbia, Quebec, and Ontario to introduce prior learning assessment and recognition services in Canada. In 1999, a national survey of Canadian prior learning assessment practices was conducted by the Canadian Association for Prior Learning Assessment (CAPLA) and funded by Human Resources Development Canada (HRD-Canada). In 2002, CAPLA received start-up funds from the Canadian Office of Learning Technologies to prepare a strategic plan for a three-year project to create an online community of practice (OCoP) that will reach and support learners, practitioners, and other stakeholders. Different forms of encouragement for provision of prior learning assessment services have been introduced in Australia, New Zealand, the Union of South Africa, and France (Evans, 2000).

In 1998, in its effort to foster implementation of principles of good practice in adult learner service, CAEL undertook a benchmarking study on adult learning focused institutions, and published a book on the results the following year (Flint & Associates, 1999). This workbook is a direct response to requests from institutions for help in evaluating their effectiveness in responding to the needs of adult learners. May it serve this purpose well!

References

Adult Degree Programs: Quality Issues, Problem Areas, and Action Steps. (1993). Chicago, IL: Council for Adult and Experiential Learning and American Council on Education.

Evans, Norman. (2000). *Experiential Learning Around the World: Employability and the Global Economy.* London: Jessica Kingsley.

Flint, Thomas A. & Associates. (1999). *Best Practices in Adult Learning: A CAEL/APQC Benchmarking Study.* New York: Forbes.

Gamson, Zelda. (1989). *Higher Education and the Real World: The Story of CAEL.* Wolfeboro, NH: Longwood Academic.

Keeton, M. T. (2002). High Points in the History of the Assessment of Experiential Learning. A working paper for the National Institute on Assessing Experiential Learning (NIAEL).

Sheckley, Barry G.; Lamdin, Lois; & Keeton, Morris T. (1993). *Employability in a High Performance Economy.* Chicago, IL: Council for Adult & Experiential Learning.

Smith, Peter. (1986). *Your Hidden Credentials: The Value of Learning Outside of College.* Washington, DC: Acropolis Books.

Stewart, David W. & Spille, Henry A. (1988). *Diploma Mills: Degrees of Fraud.* Washington, DC: American Council on Education/MacMillan.

Acknowledgments

Many people contributed to the development of this book at a variety of levels and in both direct and indirect ways. Our recognition must begin with CAEL itself. Under the leadership of President and CEO Pamela Tate, CAEL (Council for Adult and Experiential Learning) invested in the groundbreaking study of six high-performing, adult-serving institutions of higher education. The ingenuity and achievements of these six institutions were generously shared with members of CAEL's study team over a series of visits and through correspondence in early 1999. From the findings of this study, and from extensive discussion with a variety of adult educators and leaders in many sectors—higher education, business, labor unions, community-based organizations, and government—CAEL crafted the Principles of Effectiveness which are at the heart of this book. Accordingly, we thank the many people whose day-to-day involvement with adult learners in institutions, communities, and the workplace has informed this work in the years that have passed since its beginnings.

The three co-authors of this book wish to acknowledge the work of their colleagues on the original study team that resulted in the first book related to this project, *Best Practices in Adult Learning: A CAEL/APQC Benchmarking Study*. Those team members include (in alphabetical order): Marisa Brown, Sam Leiken, Kimberley Lopez, Susan Mancuso, John Strange, and Pamela Tate. We would also like to thank faculty and staff at three institutions visited specifically for the preparation of this workbook:

❖ At Governors State University:
  Freda Comer, Financial Aid
  Stuart Fagan, President
  Judy Gustawson, External Partner Liaison to the Board of Governors Program
  Joyce Harris, Lead Academic Advisor, Board of Governors BA Program
  Jagan Lingamneni, University Professor in Criminal Justice
  Becky Nugent, Writing Center Coordinator and Student Development
  Gloria Schuler, Acting Director, Board of Governors BA Degree Program
  John Stoll, Dean, Center for Extended Learning and Communications Services
  Robin Sweeney, Academic Support Counselor

❖ At Brevard Community College:
  Dorothy Campbell, Vocational Instructor
  Michele Ferrand, Financial Aid
  Carolyn Hayes, Business Professor and PLA Portfolio Evaluator
  James Heck, Dean of Educational Services, Melbourne Campus
  Roger Henry, Service Learning Director
  Janet Hrezo, Admissions
  Michael Kaliszeski, Melbourne Campus President
  David Magdaleno, Veterans Affairs
  Carol Marx, Program Advisor/Student Development Specialist
  Chandler McRee, Career Center

❖ At Regis University:

Richard Boorom, Executive Director of Marketing and New Student Enrollment
Marie Friedmann, Associate Academic Dean of Undergraduate Programs
Bill Husson, Vice President and Academic Dean
Steve Jacobs, Associate Dean
Susan Layton, Director of Operations and Administrative Services
Thomas Swanson, Director of Corporate Education Services

David Levin reviewed the Technology chapter and enriched the discussion there. Brian Tell served as editor for this publication.

Thanks belong to The Pew Charitable Trusts for their initial two-year support of the Adult Learning Focused Institution (ALFI) project. Their support enabled CAEL to disseminate findings from the study at professional conferences and workshops. Through such dissemination, many participants in the workshops we have conducted have seen early versions of the worksheets and chapters from this workbook, and their ideas and many suggestions have been incorporated into this current version.

Tom Flint, Paul Zakos & Ruth Frey
Chicago, IL
March, 2002

A NOTE TO READERS

The authors have tried to prepare this workbook knowing that it could be used in many contexts, both in the United States and internationally. For those who would like a quick start, please see page 8 in Chapter One.

Additionally, the authors appreciate that some of the terms used in this workbook have specific meanings that are not the same in all college and university settings, particularly those outside the U.S. So, to make our meanings clear, a glossary of terms can be found in Appendix F.

We welcome your thoughts and comments about this publication or about ways in which CAEL can help your institution to better serve adult learners. Please feel free to contact us at www.cael.org or 312-499-2600.

About the Authors

Thomas Flint, Ph.D.

Tom Flint is Vice President for Lifelong Learning at CAEL (Council for Adult and Experiential Learning), a non-profit association headquartered in Chicago. Since 1997, he has directed CAEL's activities in membership, publications, consulting, conferences, and Prior Learning Assessment (PLA) workshops for the higher education market. In addition, he oversees foundation funded projects such as CAEL's initiative to define and promote the Adult Learning Focused Institution. His higher education administrative experience extends over 25 years with several institutions, including Robert Morris College and DeVry, Inc. Tom's scholarly publications include articles for the *Journal of Higher Education, Research in Higher Education, Journal of College Admission*, and *Journal of Student Financial Aid*. He co-authored and edited the books *Best Practices in Adult Learning: A CAEL/APQC Benchmarking Study* and *Prior Learning Assessment: A Guidebook to American Institutional Practices*, and has made a number of presentations on this research in the US, Canada, and South Africa.

Paul Zakos

Paul Zakos has been actively involved in adult education, program and policy development, training, and human resource development since the early 1970s. He has designed and implemented education and training materials for adults in formal education settings and the workplace, and has also acted as an advisor for the development and implementation of Canadian federal and provincial policy in relation to prior learning assessment and recognition. Paul has done consulting work with the Ontario Council of Regents, the Canadian Technology Human Resources Development Board, the Forum on International Trade and Training, and the Council of Ontario Universities, among others. He is currently manager of Program Development and Prior Learning Assessment at First Nations Technical Institute in Ontario, Canada. He is also President of the Canadian Association for Prior Learning Assessment.

Ruth Frey

Ruth Frey joined CAEL in January 1999 as the Project Director for CAEL's Adult Learning Focused Institute initiative. Ruth is responsible for supporting and managing this project to develop, refine and promote principles that assure quality experiences and expanded access for adult learners. Prior to her position at CAEL, she served as the Director of Program Development at the Foundation for Independent Higher Education, where she designed and developed programs to support private colleges and universities in areas such as volunteerism, service, and inter-institutional collaboration. She has also held the position of Director for a global, long-distance doctoral program at the Association of Chicago Theological Schools. Before coming to Chicago, Ruth was the Director of Programs for the continuing education center at the Washington National Cathedral in Washington, DC, where she managed the development, marketing and implementation of programs.

Chapter 1

Why Adult Learners Matter and How You Can Help

In the title of one of his best-known books, Malcolm Knowles, the "Father of Adult Education," once called the adult learner a "neglected species." Times have changed: The adult learner is no longer neglected, though unfortunately this "species" of learner is still often mis-characterized and under-appreciated by many within higher education. A primary purpose of this workbook is to help institutions develop a better appreciation of adult learners by encouraging the adoption of policies and practices that are "adult-centered." By doing so, colleges and universities may open themselves up to becoming accessible and flexible in their continued dealings with adult students, without sacrificing any of their integrity and rigor as academic centers of higher learning. Before embarking on this venture, we will now portray what to some may be the startling dimensions of the adult student segment of the higher education enterprise.

Profiling Adult Learners in Higher Education

The abundance of adult learners in higher education is ironically matched only by the dearth of stories we hear about them through media such as newspapers and television. Nevertheless, the evidence is irrefutable that adult students have achieved normative status in higher education, at least as deserving of our attention as the stereotypical 18–23 year old student in residential, full-time study. A close look at the numbers, though, reveals the staggering proportions of adult learners to be reckoned with.

The U.S. Department of Education's National Center for Education Statistics (NCES) estimates adult student profiles within its statistical reports on the U.S. higher education population. These profiles repeatedly demonstrate the powerful presence that adult learners have on campuses. NCES studies have been conducted since 1969; in that year, it found that about 10 percent of the nation's postsecondary enrollment was in adult education (Merriam & Caffarella, 1991). By 1996–97, the NCES estimated that approximately 43 percent of the nation's 14 million postsecondary education students were 25 years of age or older. The most astonishing growth in enrollments occurred between 1985–86 and 1996–97 for adult students 35 years and older—an estimated 65 percent increase, from 1.7 million to 2.9 million (Hussar, 1998). An earlier NCES report frankly declaimed, "Not since the 1970s has the typical student in postsecondary education been a recent high school graduate enrolled full time in a 4-year college or university, working toward a bachelor's degree. On the contrary, these students represented about one-third of undergraduates enrolled in 1992–93" (Horn & Premo, 1995, p. 1).

Adult students are loosely identified with a larger group characterized as "non-traditional." While definitions vary according to the user, the seven characteristics defining the non-traditional student within a recent NCES study closely corresponds to common traits shared by many students over 24 years or age ("adult" by the age criterion):

❖ Delayed enrollment into post-secondary education;
❖ Attending part-time;
❖ Financially independent;
❖ Working full-time while enrolled;
❖ Having dependents other than a spouse;
❖ Being a single parent; or
❖ Not having a standard high school diploma.

(Horn & Carroll, 1996, pp. 3–7)

Clearly, many students under 25 might exhibit one or more of these traits. Also, age alone cannot be cause for attributing the label "adult" when we mean to denote persons with life circumstances requiring social independence, commitments to family and work, and personal identities that have evolved beyond that of full-time student. While the law in many localities may recognize adulthood at age 18, when we refer to "adult" learners in this book, we refer to those students whose lives are typified by circumstances such as those listed above, though we count "adults" by using the simplified criterion of age alone.

Explicit comparisons reveal important differences in characteristics and behaviors of U.S. adult students compared with traditional aged students (18–23 years). As summarized by the NCES:

❖ In 1989–90, 42 percent of all undergraduates were 24 years or older (39 percent of males and 45 percent of females).
❖ In contrast to their younger counterparts, the majority of older undergraduates were married (56 percent compared with 7 percent) and had dependents other than a spouse (53 percent compared with 4 percent). One-quarter of all female undergraduates in their 30s were single parents.
❖ Older undergraduates were predominantly part-time students. Only 31 percent attended full time (in contrast to 73 percent of younger undergraduates).
❖ Forty-six percent of all older undergraduates worked full time while enrolled. They were more likely than younger undergraduates to work full time regardless of whether they were enrolled full time or part time.
❖ Among older undergraduates, only sixteen percent of those who worked full time received financial aid from their employers.
❖ About three-quarters of the older undergraduates who enrolled in postsecondary education for the first time in 1989–90 perceived themselves primarily as workers rather than students.

(Choy, Premo & Maw 1995, p. iii)

Many of these characteristics and behaviors are well known and have typified adult learners for many years (Cross, 1979). Prominent among past findings is the fact that adult learners are frequently motivated to study for career- or work-related reasons. At the same time, higher education institutions are but one type of an entire range of service providers offering education and training to adults in order to augment their workplace skills. Much of what we refer to as "adult education" obtained for work-related reasons is not learning at the college or university level, but rather consists of activities such as language or literacy skills training.

In 1995, NCES published a report that examined that year's National Household Education Survey for the purpose of estimating U.S. adults' participation in work-related courses. The analysts found that about forty percent of employed adults participated in work-related adult education. Narrowing the focus to participation in work-related courses, the researchers report among their key findings that:

❖ The overall participation rate in work-related courses was 22 percent in 1994–95.

❖ College graduates were more than twice as likely as persons who completed only high school to participate in work-related courses during the 12 months prior to the interview (39 percent and 18 percent, respectively).

❖ Adults between the ages of 26 and 54 years were almost twice as likely to participate in work-related courses compared to the youngest or oldest adults (27 percent versus 16 percent).

❖ Women constituted half of the participants in work-related courses.

❖ Rates of participation in work-related courses were generally higher among persons in professional or managerial occupations (ranging from 41 percent to 71 percent) and lower among those in trades (ranging from 11 percent to 22 percent).

❖ Nearly half of all participants (48 percent) took work-related courses provided by business and industry. Other providers included educational institutions (elementary, secondary, and postsecondary) and professional and trade associations.

❖ Time (47 percent) and cost (30 percent) were the most frequently reported barriers to participation in work-related courses by interested populations.

(Darkenwald & Kim, 1998, pp. 1–2)

Population estimates for these adults in work-related courses reveal staggering numbers. Though instructional providers take the form of business, industry, and professional organizations that serve well over half of their number, in the U.S. there are 39.6 million adults whom we may regard as "lifelong learners", of whom:

❖ 2.5 million are taking work-related courses in community colleges;

❖ 900,000 are in public two-year vocational and technical schools;

❖ 4 million are in private vocational, trade, business, flight, or hospitals schools; and

❖ 4.9 million are in four-year colleges and universities.

(Darkenwald & Kim, 1998, p. 13)

Some recent evidence suggests that an 'echo' of the 'baby boom' might soon be rippling through U.S. higher education (Carnevale & Frye, 2000). However, a study of students over the age of 40 suggests that this group will continue to occupy a strong presence on U.S. campuses (*Life After 40*, 1996). Among the key findings of the study:

❖ Students over 40 are rapidly increasing as a proportion of the total enrollment in formal higher education;

❖ Increasing educational requirements for employment, changing life circumstances, and personal growth are primary factors motivating the entrance or return to post-secondary education by adults over 40;

❖ Surveys of workers reveal that those over 40 have the greatest need for training in their current jobs;

❖ Students over 40 must contend with a range of complex issues that can have an impact on their ability to pursue or succeed in post-secondary education;

❖ Many students over the age of 40 have difficulty taking advantage of student services designed to assist them; and

❖ Students over 40 are key factors driving innovative approaches to post-secondary education and training.

(Life After 40, 1996, pp. 14–17)

The U.S. experience with growth in adult enrollments is being experienced worldwide (Davies, 1995). Kasworm (1993) reports that in the developed nations such as Canada, Finland, and

Germany, the percentage of adults in postsecondary education more than doubled between 1981 and 1990.

In many respects, though the 'face' of the typical student in higher education has changed in recent decades, the 'face' of policies and practices at institutions of higher education has not. This workbook is intended to help institutions discover some of the limitations of traditional policies and practices when applied to adult learners, while imagining new possibilities and innovations for serving adults.

CAEL's Role in Promoting Adult Learning

Many colleges and universities have struggled to adapt to this changing student marketplace, often finding themselves burdened by traditions and practices that prove ill-suited for adults. Adult students have unique needs, especially if they are employed. Among others, these needs include:

* ❖ Different kinds of information about their educational options;
* ❖ Institutional flexibility in curricula and support services;
* ❖ Academic and motivational advising supportive of their life and career goals; and
* ❖ Recognition of experience- and work-based learning already obtained.

These needs reflect how the experience, knowledge, skills, and attitudes of adult learners are different from those of traditional aged students. However, without good models of effective practice for serving adult learners, colleges and universities will continue to struggle. CAEL* (Council for Adult and Experiential Learning) has addressed this issue through an initiative designed to assist colleges and universities with improving learning opportunities for working adults.

CAEL partnered with APQC (American Productivity & Quality Center) to conduct a CAEL benchmarking study of six highly adult learning focused colleges and universities. This was a first step toward identifying and disseminating new models of how higher education institutions can provide the best possible educational experience for adult students. CAEL's study is published in book form, titled *Best Practices in Adult Learning* (Flint & Associates, 1999).

CAEL then transformed the benchmarking study findings into principles of effective practice that have been further tested within focus groups of adult learners, educators, employers, union representatives, policy makers, and others who are interested in adult learning. These Principles of Effectiveness for Serving Adult Learners describe processes and approaches to be adopted by colleges seeking to improve access by, and quality for, adult students. However, in order to assure flexibility and innovation by institutions, the Principles do not prescribe particular practices or policies. Rather, they are meant to serve as a framework for assessing institutional commitment to, and capacity for, meeting the needs of adults, and also to form the backbone of what CAEL calls the Adult Learning Focused Institution (ALFI).

Principles of Effectiveness for Serving Adult Learners

The following table shows the eight Principles and their definitions:

Table 1.1 Principles and Definitions

Outreach	The institution conducts its outreach to adult learners by overcoming barriers of time, place, and tradition in order to create lifelong access to educational opportunities.
Life and Career Planning	The institution addresses adult learners' life and career goals before or at the onset of enrollment in order to assess and align its capacities to help learners reach their goals.
Financing	The institution promotes choice using an array of payment options for adult learners in order to expand equity and financial flexibility.
Assessment of Learning Outcomes	The institution defines and assesses the knowledge, skills, and competencies acquired by adult learners both from the curriculum and from life/work experience in order to assign credit and confer degrees with rigor.
Teaching-Learning Process	The institution's faculty uses multiple methods of instruction (including experiential and problem-based methods) for adult learners in order to connect curricular concepts to useful knowledge and skills.
Student Support Systems	The institution assists adult learners using comprehensive academic and student support systems in order to enhance students' capacities to become self-directed, lifelong learners.
Technology	The institution uses information technology to provide relevant and timely information and to enhance the learning experience.
Strategic Partnerships	The institution engages in strategic relationships, partnerships, and collaborations with employers and other organizations in order to develop and improve educational opportunities for adult learners.

The purpose of this workbook is not to show how to replicate the CAEL benchmarking study nor to describe how to validate the Principles in your local context. Rather, this workbook is focused on assisting institutions with implementing the Principles.

Approaches to Institutional Improvement

Though it makes for inspirational story telling, heroic action by solitary individuals rarely changes the nature of institutions or organizations. The collective thinking and habits of people in institutional contexts exert a powerful braking action against new attitudes and behavior, over which one person alone cannot prevail. Accordingly, in this workbook we assume that although a change initiative may start with a single person (perhaps you, the reader), it will not end there. In this workbook we shall refer to the Change Leaders Project Team, a group of people at your institution who will champion the initiatives on behalf of adult learners.

Using steps outlined in this workbook beginning in the next chapter (Chapter 2—'How to Get Started'), the Change Leaders Project Team may initiate, develop, and direct the efforts spread across many people at the institution to better serve adults. As such, this team may function as a relatively autonomous and potentially permanent committee devoted to improving adult learning practices at your campus. Chapter 2 identifies some important issues in the recruitment, selection, and management of this team both for its short- and long-term operation. Clearly, effective facilitation of the team will be crucial to its success. Consider carefully how well facilitated teams and committees tend to operate at your institution. While some institutions do this well, the sad reality is that many institutions do this poorly.

One option to consider is the value of using an outside consultant to facilitate the processes described in this workbook. An outside facilitator may be free of the biases, politics, or constraints that might otherwise hinder an 'insider' whose future is tied to the institution. Additionally, outside facilitators may bring invaluable experience or perspectives beyond that of individual members of the Change Leaders Project Team—in effect, "thinking outside the box" may be best facilitated by one who actually works "outside the box." For a number of years, CAEL has provided consultation and facilitation to institutions of higher education around innovative adult learning processes. Because of its continuing investment in the ALFI project, CAEL will readily enter a discussion about how its intervention might further the efforts of your Change Leaders Project Team in building your institution into an ALFI.

If you would like to request CAEL's assistance, contact:

The ALFI Project
CAEL (Council for Adult & Experiential Learning)
55 East Monroe, Suite 1930
Chicago, Illinois 60603
USA
Phone (312) 499-2600
Website: www.cael.org

Critical Success Factors

Before undertaking the institutional self-assessment activities in this workbook, we encourage you to recognize some fundamental groundwork that may be essential in order to for you to achieve your goals. Your first step to launch a new effort in the right direction, especially one that must draw upon expertise and information that might be spread widely across the institution, may be your biggest challenge. So we urge you to pay attention to the vital signs we identify in this chapter.

The critical success factors discussed below will be revisited in more detail in Chapter 12, "How Well Are You Doing?" Our purpose in introducing them here is to alert you to their presence and to encourage you to plan ahead to summon the best personal and institutional assets you have at your disposal around each of these factors. Later, as you work with your colleagues, and as the progress on the institutional self-assessment unfolds, use the list to check the level of energy and momentum necessary to keep propelling you and your colleagues forward. If you sense that energy and purpose is flagging, you may want to look at the following list of factors and see if one of them is at play.

In our view, effective problem solving activity within institutions and organizations hinges upon the following factors. To begin, the problem must be:

➤ *Consequential*—Skeptics may abound. They may ask, "Why bother?" You may need to gather the evidence, either at the outset or along the way, that achieving your goals will have an important impact—to create "a difference that makes a difference."

➤ *Persistent*—Like a rain delay at a ballgame, some problems go away by themselves. In contrast, be ready to work with your colleagues in order to show them that for a persistent problem, doing nothing is not a solution.

➤ *Understood by Stakeholders*—Be prepared to speak using concepts and language that everyone understands. You may find it important to draw parallels to a well-understood event from the institution's history, around which there is consensus about this past problem, solution, and outcome.

➤ *Unresolved*—Have past remedies fallen short? As the old quip states, insanity may be defined as doing the same thing over and over again, yet believing that a different result will occur. The strongest case for new solutions is advanced when it is clear that the old solutions no longer suffice.

➤ *Urgent*—Those who work with adult learners know that adult students often present themselves to the institution as being in a hurry to accomplish their goals. One of your tasks in working with your colleagues will be to convey some of this same sense of urgency around your institution's improvement of efforts to serve adults.

Besides these features of the problem situation, consider some important organizational factors:

➤ *Leadership*—Who champions the cause? Leadership takes a variety of forms and faces; will your effort have the right ones?

➤ *Adaptability*—Where there are the fewest barriers, there may be the greatest success. Scan your institutional environment for those places that are likely to have the least number of policies and regulations that could hamper your efforts, and where early successes—no matter how small—will boost the morale of people sharing your goals.

➤ *Resources*—Time and money are precious commodities to adult learners. Without doubt, they are also precious to your institution. Devote part of your time to finding resources that could be marshaled for the changes needed to better serve adult learners.

➤ *Shared Values*—Colleges and universities are communities rich in diversity. To leverage action by the community or a significant part of it, though, requires some shared sentiments and goals. Otherwise, there is no ownership of the problem to be addressed. Be prepared to invoke the shared values that inspire action on the part of the institution.

Your institution will be unusually fortunate to have a perfect alignment of all of these factors working on your behalf. More likely, one or more of the factors will point to a challenge that you and your colleagues must address if progress is to be achieved. Start your efforts with a clear view of the potential obstacles in your path and some strategies to bypass them.

Getting Started

In general, we wish to discourage paralysis by analysis. Knowing that there are some critical factors to keep in mind while beginning to proceed as best as you can is, in our view, preferable to delaying in the false hope of concocting a perfect plan. In the next two chapters, we outline some important preparatory steps. Then, each Principle of Effectiveness is presented in a dedicated chapter, with further description of the Principle in both meaning and action. Each Principle is illustrated by actual institutional examples of the Principle at work, and each chapter closes with an associated worksheet for you to use during the process of institutional self-assessment. Finally, we close the book with chapters containing ideas about summarizing your assessment outcomes, trouble-shooting problems, and learning from stories of colleges and universities that have successfully integrated these Principles into their adult learning programs.

Are You Eager for a Quick Start?

Appendix C provides you with a slide show to help explain purposes and activities of this workbook (page 127).

Appendix D consolidates all of the Worksheets used in the book (page 141).

Appendix E contains implementation tools (page 151).

Appendix F is a Glossary of special terms used in the Workbook and on the Worksheets (page 155).

References

Carnevale, Anthony P. & Frye, Richard. (2000). *Crossing the Great Divide*. Princeton, NJ: Educational Testing Service.

Choy, S.P.; Premo, M.K.; & Maw, C. (1995). *Profile of Older Undergraduates: 1989–90*. NCES Report 95–167. Washington, DC: Office of Educational Research and Improvement, U.S. Department of Education.

Cross, K.P. (1979). Adult learners: Characteristics, needs, and interests. In R. E. Peterson & Associates. *Lifelong Learning in America*. San Francisco: Jossey-Bass.

Darkenwald, Gorden & Kim, Kwang. (1998). *Adults' Participation in Work-Related Courses: 1994–95*, NCES Report 98-309. Washington, DC: U.S. Department of Education, National Center for Education Statistics.

Davies, Pat (ed.) (1995). *Adults in Higher Education: International Perspectives in Access and Participation*. Bristol, PA: Jessica Kingsley Publishers.

Flint, Thomas A. & Associates. (1999). *Best Practices in Adult Learning: A CAEL/APQC Benchmarking Study*. Chicago, IL: Council for Adult and Experiential Learning.

Horn, Laura J. & Carroll, C. Dennis. (1996). *Nontraditional Undergraduates: Trends in Enrollment from 1986 to 1992 and Persistence and Attainment Among 1989–90 Beginning Postsecondary Students*. NCES Report 97-578. Washington, DC: Office of Educational Research and Improvement, U.S. Department of Education.

Horn, Laura J. and Premo, Mark D. (1995). *Profile of Undergraduates in U.S. Postsecondary Education Institutions: 1992–93*. NCES Report 96-237. Washington, DC: Office of Educational Research and Improvement, U.S. Department of Education.

Hussar, William J. (1998).   *Projections of Education Statistics to 2008.* NCES Report 98-017. Washington, DC: Office of Educational Research and Improvement, U.S. Department of Education.

Kasworm, Carol.   (1993).   Adult higher education from an international perspective.   *Higher Education,* 25 (June), 411-423.

Life After 40: A New Portrait of Today's—and Tomorrow's—Postsecondary Students. (1996). Research report, The Education Resources Institute and Institute for Higher Education Policy, October, 1996.

Merriam, Sharan B. and Caffarella, Rosemary S. (1991).   *Learning in Adulthood: A Comprehensive Guide.* San Francisco: Jossey-Bass Publishers.

Chapter 2

How to Get Started

Purpose of This Workbook

The purpose of this workbook is to serve as a guide for those who wish to help their institutions become more adult learning focused. It has been designed specifically to assist you in gaining the institutional support needed to put in place significant changes which more fully adapt to the changing demographics of the higher education population and to strengthen your institution's services to adult learners. In so doing, it provides you with some of the content, tools, and information necessary for you to achieve the following outcomes:

1. Informally assess your institution's services to adult learners.

2. Locate and mobilize vital institutional and community support and the resources needed to identify and close gaps in service to adult learners at your institution.

This workbook is intended to be a guide. The responsibility will be on you and your colleagues to decide which areas need attention and to develop strategies to address the most important priorities. Each of the eight key *Principles of Effectiveness*, their accompanying Best Practice Performance Indicators, and the specific institutional examples are dealt with in detail in separate chapters of this workbook. Included for each of the key *Principles of Effectiveness* and the accompanying Best Practice Performance Indicators is an informal, institutional self-assessment process. There are also some suggestions about how to generate evidence to document your institution's performance in serving adult learners, ways to gather institutional and community support, and the resources necessary to strengthen existing services and fill gaps in service.

This workbook is based on the premise that people learn best by doing and reflecting upon what happened. Other assumptions about learning also support the content, structure, and processes described in this workbook. They are as follows:

1. You are in charge of this institutional self-assessment process and its results. You will shape the content, process, and tools offered in this workbook by your own experiences, values, and views of adult learners, the learning process and the universe of higher education.

2. You will bring into this activity those resources and ideas that enable you to influence change in the areas that most fit your experiences, values, and beliefs about the ways in which adult learners are treated at your institution. Generally, you will respond to what is familiar to you and directions in this workbook are meant to be taken as suggestions. You may also have other strategies and techniques for implementing change that have worked for you in the past. We urge you to draw upon them as well.

3. You will bypass those processes and resources described in this workbook that you view as being unnecessary or irrelevant in terms of helping your institution to become more adult learning focused.

The information and activities included in this workbook may perform other important functions. First, they may strengthen your commitment to advocate for critical changes on behalf of adult learners, and to act in collaboration with adult learners and colleagues inside and outside of your institution. Second, they may raise your awareness of the key *Principles of Effectiveness* formulated by CAEL as an outcome of the CAEL Benchmarking Study. The activities suggested throughout this workbook may be viewed as being important components of a larger, continuous improvement process which involves discarding outdated assumptions and misconceptions about adult learners, and adopting new ideas, beliefs, practices, and processes that are more timely and relevant. Our challenge is to provide you with the best possible resources and support in your efforts to help your institution to serve adult learners in a more individualized, timely, flexible, efficient, and cost-effective manner.

The workbook activities are also intended to be participatory and action-oriented. It is our desire to assist you with diagnosing the existing strengths and gaps in service to adults at your own institution as accurately as possible. The informal institutional self-assessment tool is an important first step in that process. A second major step is to either acquire or enhance the skills, knowledge and resources needed to plan and implement a process to meet the identified needs. A third step is to capitalize on the existing skills, knowledge, and experiences of key members of your institution and your community to help develop and implement requisite changes in services to adult learners. If you decide to design and implement a strategy to help your institution become more adult learning focused, the sections that follow should help you formulate some important questions about how you might like to proceed.

As you begin to implement the activities outlined in this workbook and adapt them to the unique interests, needs, characteristics, and processes of your institution, you may find the following questions helpful:

1. *Prior to mobilizing institutional and community support to close identified service gaps to adult learners:*

    - **What makes this particular goal appropriate at this time?**

    - **What changes do you hope to make and what will be the implications for the institution, adult learners, and the community?**

2. *After implementing your strategy for institutional change:*

    - **How have your perceptions, beliefs and attitudes changed (i.e. what have you learned) after taking these actions?**

    - **Has the way in which your institution provides services to adult learners changed for the better?**

    - **What evidence do you have that this is the case?**

The Change Leaders Project Team

One of the most important considerations in taking on the challenging task of helping your institution become more adult learning focused is the issue of how to get the ball rolling. Prior to embarking on the informal, institutional self-assessment process advocated in this workbook, it is important that you realize the complexities involved in institutional change processes. While there is little doubt that highly motivated and determined individuals can often have a significant impact on organizational policies and processes, such a task is best tackled using a team-based approach. Early in the process, it will be valuable to consider forming a team as the main vehicle to help initiate desired modifications in the way your institution helps adult learners meet their educational goals.

The process of diagnosing strengths and gaps in service to adult learners, developing action plans, and implementing and evaluating changes to improve services requires time, energy, insight and commitment from a variety of key change leaders from within the organization and a few select individuals from outside of the institution. The task of effecting significant change in complex organizations such as colleges and universities is often too great for one individual no matter how motivated or talented.

One suggestion is to assemble a Change Leaders Project Team, the members of which could be recruited from all departments/stakeholders within the institution, i.e. administration, the adult learner student body, faculty, support and clerical staff. In addition, other team members could be drawn from specific stakeholder groups external to the institution such as alumni, business, labor and community leaders.

TIP

The Change Leaders Project Team must represent diverse offices and stakeholders for your institution's operation. Your efforts for institutional improvement may stall or stop if:

◆ Lack of information makes the self-evaluation questions impossible to answer fairly or accurately. Try to get as many of "the right people in the room" as possible before beginning the worksheet exercises.

◆ Lack of authority or expertise makes the implementation planning impractical or impossible to deliver. Imagining work that absent people should perform to address the problems identified is a fruit-less exercise.

Membership on the Change Leaders Project Team should be strictly voluntary. Members should share a common belief in the need for, and the desire to bring about, positive change in the way the institution responds to adult learners. Members should also be familiar with and committed to using the key *Principles of Effectiveness* as their road map to chart a path of continuous improvement of services to adult learners. The team should meet regularly to review its practices, assess needs, identify areas for improvement, set goals and priorities, locate resources, create action plans, and implement the needed changes. The team should also be responsible for assessing the outcomes of any changes made. This process is cyclical in nature and could be repeated throughout the academic year. It represents what the Japanese refer to as *kaizan* or continuous improvement.

The benefits of such a team-based approach are many. A few of the more significant benefits include the following:

1. A more accurate assessment and understanding of the challenges which the Best Practices Performance Indicators pose for specific departments in shaping the Adult Learning

Focused Institution. Initial changes may have a ripple effect on other departments and the external constituencies served by the institution.

2. Increased participation and sense of ownership by a wider variety of institutional and community leaders. Energy and satisfaction may grow from the problem-solving and decision-making processes relating to how the institution meets its ongoing obligations and responsibilities to its adult learner population.

3. Enhanced skills and knowledge. Team members and others will be able to assess the impact of changes on faculty, staff, students, departments, the community-at-large, labor unions and employers.

4. The opportunity to demonstrate to the institution the ways in which the continuous improvement process enables it to respond positively to changing needs and societal conditions.

Establishing the Team—Membership, Dynamics

If you decide to take some action to help your institution become more Adult Learning Focused with the use of the team-based approach advocated in this workbook, it may be helpful to consider developing the Change Leaders Project Team in two phases.

The initial phase is best described as the pre-implementation stage, which involves reaching out to key institutional and community leaders to determine their interest in participating in the implementation initiative. It seems reasonable to assume that most, if not all, of the members of the pre-implementation team will form the core of the team to eventually implement needed changes in services to adult learners at your institution. However, as you begin a process of helping to educate your institution and the community about the aims and outcomes of your work, you may encounter individuals along the way who have the necessary energy and commitment to play a significant role in the implementation process. Also, original members may decide to leave the team for a variety of reasons.

It is important to be mindful of the fact that in the early stages of the pre-implementation process, there will be differences in perception among team members about the challenges at hand. For example, there may be divergent views about the capacity, resources and motivation to change on the part of specific areas or departments within your institution. Encouraging all team members to openly share their perceptions and opinions as early as possible in the process should enable you to quickly "take the pulse" of your institution in relation to its services to adults.

Once membership on the pre-implementation team has been determined and initial reactions have been aired, a useful starting point is to initiate a focused dialogue among team members. They should be encouraged to share their interests, needs, and capabilities in relation to the challenges that such an initiative presents. You will also need to spend time sharing perspectives, potential strategies, and solutions to help your institution improve its services to adults.

Developing the Team

Depending upon the size of the team, you may wish to consider implementing the activities which follow either in one large group (6–10 participants), or two or three smaller ones (3–4 participants). Should you decide to pursue this activity in small groups, it will be important to have each group select a recorder and spokesperson. These people will capture the main points of the discussion, and record and report them to all team members in a general session at the end of the activity.

As part of the team development process, make sure that all team members have an opportunity to help shape the agenda for any implementation activities within your institution. You might begin by asking each member of the team to share his/her background, interests, skills and expectations in relation to the project. For example:

1.   What do they hope that the project will achieve?

2.   What role(s) would they like to play in the process?

3.   What fears and concerns do they have?

4.   What are some of the obstacles that they believe will need to be overcome?

5.   What are some of the strategies and resources that will contribute to a successful project?

The issues and questions outlined above are meant as general guidelines and suggestions. They are designed to help you formulate questions and strategies that are tailored to the unique needs and culture of your institution, as well as the strengths, interests, resources, and energy of the members of your team.

This chapter has outlined the reasons for the development of this workbook, the ways in which it can be used, and the desired outcomes. It has also advocated for the use of a project team of leaders drawn from across the institution and key stakeholders from the community as the main vehicle to mobilize and implement the resources and support needed to change the way your institution serves adult learners.

The next chapter discusses the informal institutional self-assessment process. It identifies the processes, principles, and tools needed to systematically assess your institution's services to adult learners.

Focusing Your Attention: 'Wide' or 'Narrow'?

Should your evaluation focus upon the entire institution, or upon one or more units within it, such as a school, college, department, or program? There is no one right answer to this question that applies suitably in all situations. Here are some considerations that are relevant to your decision:

◆ The Principles of Effectiveness address adult students' experiences of the institution as a whole, not merely selected bits and pieces. The findings from CAEL's benchmarking study show that for high-performing, adult-serving institutions, the Principles are indivisible if you wish to assure effective service to adults. If you choose not to evaluate the entire institution, will the unit or units you assess demonstrate a scope of activity—and an appropriate ability to influence outcomes—across the entire set of Principles?

◆ In very large or complex institutions, the people you need to answer the questions embedded in the worksheets in this book may be dispersed widely across the institution. Will you be able to secure their participation?

◆ You may already know or suspect that institutional performance relative to the Principles is quite inconsistent across the offices or departments that serve adults, or may be quite uneven in quality within those units. In this case, be clear about the situation that you wish to illuminate and the problems that you wish to address.

◆ Individual units (schools, colleges, departments, or programs) within the institution may differ greatly in their current and anticipated adult student enrollment. Be sensitive not only to where currently enrolled adults experience the institution, but where future adult students may be enrolled. For example, a unit that does not have many adults at the moment might, nonetheless, be expected to see a large influx in the future, based on changes in the external environment.

We will return to this question in Chapter 3, "Selecting an Area of Focus." As you grapple with the considerations listed above, keep these questions in mind: **If you choose not to focus upon the entire institution, which adult learners may be compromised by your decision to narrow the focus? Why should their potential interests be excluded?**

Whatever your final choice may be—the institution as a whole or units therein—do not lose sight of your definition of *institution* as discussion proceeds in this workbook about the Adult Learning Focused Institution.

References

Ankarlo, Loren. (1997). *9 Traits of Highly Successful Work Teams*. St. Catharines, ON: CareerTrack.

Elledge, Robin L. and Phillips, Steven L. (1997). *Team Building for the Future*. Scarborough, ON: Jossey-Bass/Pfeiffer.

Devine, Irene and Dimock, Hedley G. (1996). *Managing Dynamic Groups*, 3rd Edition. North York, ON: Captus Press.

Hollingworth, D.A. (1996). *Teams and Work Groups*. Mississauga, ON: The Gencor Group Inc.

Johnson, David W. and Johnson, Frank P. (1999). *Joining Together, Group Theory and Group Skills*, 7th Edition. Needham Heights, MA: Allyn and Bacon Publishers.

Chapter 3

How to Proceed

This chapter describes in detail the informal institutional self-assessment process. It also

- ❖ outlines the basic steps involved in performing the assessment; and
- ❖ illustrates key elements needed to collect concrete evidence to document how well your institution serves adult learners as compared to CAEL's eight key *Principles of Effectiveness*.

These self-assessment tools, principles, and processes will enable you to identify ways in which you can strengthen existing services to adult learners, minimize the negative impact of restraining forces, and fill any gaps. The self-assessment process that follows will enable you to determine systematically your institution's performance in relation to CAEL's eight *Principles of Effectiveness*.

Selecting an Area of Focus

It is possible to use this self-assessment process to ascertain the performance of an individual school within a larger institutional structure or indeed to assess the performance of a single program within a school or department of an institution. However, one of the major premises of the CAEL Benchmarking Study is that at an Adult Learning Focused Institution (ALFI) **all** adult learners, regardless of the institution, school, college, or department in which they are registered, should have equal access to every service offered by that institution. A second major premise of the CAEL Benchmarking Study is that **all** services, regardless of their location within the institution, should be delivered to adult learners in an individualized, flexible, timely, convenient, collaborative, and cost-effective manner. Helping some adult learners meet their education goals and aspirations in one part of the institution—while simultaneously denying adults such services in other parts of the same institution—contributes to an uneven playing field for learners. Unfortunately, this unevenness currently characterizes services to adult learners in scores of institutions and across entire systems of higher education.

The worksheets have been designed to help you compare, as directly as possible, the current practices utilized at your institution in serving adult learners to the eight key *Principles of Effectiveness* and their Best Practice Performance Indicators which emerged from the ALFI Study. The list of Best Practice Performance Indicators that accompany each of the Key *Principles of Effectiveness* does not necessarily represent all of the performance indicators for each of the principles. There may be others that you are able to identify from your own experiences working with adult learners. Please feel free to add them to any of the existing lists.

As you review each of the eight key *Principles of Effectiveness* and their Performance Indicators you may notice some overlap, especially in relation to the Performance Indicators. One of the reasons for this is that many of the Principles combine to form an integrated approach to serving adult learners. They are best seen as being important elements in a continuum of services rather than as separate and distinct tasks. For example, Outreach, Student Support Systems and Life and Career Planning are so tightly woven into the fabric of services provided by high performing ALFIs that at any given time it may be difficult to differentiate one of these principles from the others.

To illustrate this process, ALFIs utilize outreach to adults as the beginning of the educational planning and student support processes. The important dialogue that is initiated as part of the outreach process inevitably involves the examination of educational hopes, aspirations and goals, the need for personal and academic support, and a variety of other issues, many of which are identified at the point of first contact with adult learners. The integrated approach exemplified by ALFIs minimizes the negative impact that compartmentalized and fragmented services often have on adult learners. In administering the process of education, the boundaries that define where one departmental service stops and another begins can represent major hurdles for adult learners. ALFIs exhibit a keen sensitivity to such barriers and work hard to ensure that adult learners do not fall into service gaps at their institutions.

Performing the Informal Institutional Self-Assessment

This section outlines the basic steps and principles involved in assessing your institution's services to adult learners. The eight key *Principles of Effectiveness* and the self-assessment categories are listed along with a description of how to use the self-assessment scale. As you embark upon the institutional self-assessment process (Chapters 4–11) it may be useful to bear in mind the over-arching theme resulting from the original CAEL Benchmarking Study: "The Adult Learning Focused Institution has a culture in which adult-centered learning, sensitivity to learners' needs, flexibility, and communication drive constitutional practice."

The eight key *Principles of Effectiveness*, their Performance Indicators and specific institutional examples have been crafted to enable you to determine, as objectively as possible, the extent to which your institution embodies such a culture.

Using the Self-Assessment Scale

Carefully review each of the eight key *Principles of Effectiveness* and the Best Practice Performance Indicators that exemplify their application (Chapters 4–11). Using the institutional self-assessment scale in each chapter, record what you think is the present level of performance at your institution, in terms of its services to adult learners for each of the key Principles. Place a mark in the column Y (Yes), N (No) or UD (Under Development) that best describes your institution's current performance in that area. In the next column make note of the unit (or person) responsible for the Principle that is being assessed and the name of the individual in charge of the unit.

Make notes of possible sources of documentation in the right hand (Evidence) column. List particular items such as mission statements, recruitment and instructional materials, websites, etc. made available to adult learners which could be used to provide concrete evidence of your institution's performance as compared to the eight key Principles of Effectiveness.

The eight Principles discussed in Chapter 4 through 11 include Outreach, Life and Career Planning, Financing, Assessment of Learning Outcomes, Teaching-Learning Process, Student Support Systems, Technology and Strategic Partnerships.

Collecting Evidence to Support Best Practice Performance

Throughout the informal institutional self-assessment process, be sure to emphasize the importance of using diverse sources of evidence. We strongly recommend finding at least three sources for each of the eight key *Principles of Effectiveness*.

In gathering evidence, you may find that pockets of Best Practice Performance Indicators exist in some departments or areas of the institution. However, it is important to keep in mind that while such practices are positive indicators that the Principles exist, they may not be readily accessible to all adult learners at your institution. Significant gaps in service identified as a result of the informal institutional assessment can help you to set some priorities and to develop action plans to fill the gaps, should you and your team decide to do so.

Figure One, for example, illustrates some of the diverse types of tangible evidence that may be available at your institution to document its performance related to the Teaching/Learning Process.

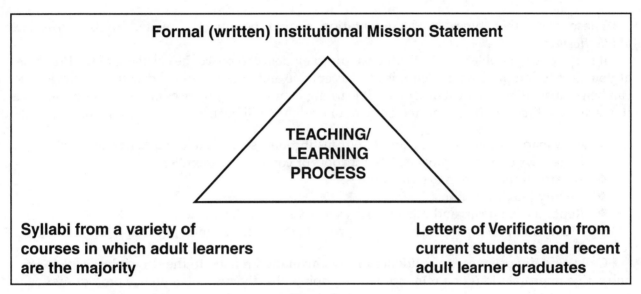

Figure One

You may also need to identify several examples of evidence. For example, you might initially find a piece of evidence—such as an official press release by the institution's Board of Governors or President which affirms its commitment to serving its adult learner population—that demonstrates your institution's commitment to serving adult learners for several of the key Principles. However, such an announcement by itself would not be sufficient to indicate the existence of any of the key *Principles of Effectiveness*. Generally, it is suggested that you provide more than one source of evidence to demonstrate your institution's commitment to adult learners for each of the Principles. Providing diverse sources of evidence lends greater objectivity to the informal institutional self-assessment process. It should also enable you to more reliably and accurately identify areas of strength and gaps in services.

Generating tangible evidence is an integral component of the institutional self-assessment activity. Ideally, the best evidence is that which is directly related to one or more of the *Principles of Effectiveness* and their Best Practice Performance Indicators. It will be important, then, to base the assessment less on personal judgment and perceptions and more on the accumulation of "hard," i.e. direct, concrete evidence related to the Principles. Examples of direct evidence are many and varied. They may include:

❖   Student feedback from surveys, letters, petitions, and similar sources;
❖   Annual reports from departments or schools;
❖   Samples of plans implemented;
❖   Suggestions adopted to improve services;

- ❖ Learning outcomes specified;
- ❖ Course objectives and class schedules;
- ❖ Verification or testimonial letters from adult learners;
- ❖ Results from evaluation instruments that provide feedback to faculty and/or the administration;
- ❖ Audio visual presentations;
- ❖ Books and publications;
- ❖ Faculty training manuals; or
- ❖ Advisory committee membership and minutes.

These and other types of documentation should be directly related to the *Principles of Effectiveness*.

It may not be possible to collect sufficient direct evidence to prove the existence of the Principles at your institution. Indirect evidence is also acceptable and, when combined with direct evidence, can help substantiate the existence of adult learning focused best practices at your institution. As is the case with direct evidence, indirect sources of evidence will be many, diverse, and could include:

- ❖ Newspaper articles written about your institution's services to adult learners;
- ❖ Letters written by employers, labor leaders or community members;
- ❖ Awards received from external bodies;
- ❖ Faculty job descriptions;
- ❖ Reports from deans and other senior executives of the institution; or
- ❖ Membership in organizations which promote the adult learning agenda.

Collecting diverse pieces of evidence or documentation related to the Principles helps to keep subjective interpretations to a minimum. In so doing, the diversity of evidence provides you and your team with a reasonably accurate and realistic picture of the services that your institution is providing to the adults in your community. An enlightened approach to the institutional self-assessment also takes into account the challenges to objectivity faced by all those performing assessments of any type. Some of these challenges are worth noting as part of this workbook. In fact, there are some who speculate that all measurement, including the most specific and behavioral, is ultimately subjective in nature. For example, the renowned psychologist Carl Rogers had these observations:

> Man lives essentially in his own personal and subjective world and even his most objective functioning in science, mathematics, and the like is the result of subjective purpose and subjective choice. Though there may be such thing as objective truth, I can never know it; all I can know is that some statements appear to me subjectively to have the qualifications of objective truth. (Rogers, C. A Theory of Therapy, Personality and Interpersonal Relationships. In S. Koch (Ed.), Psychology: A Study of a Science (Vol. 3). New York, McGraw Hill, 1959. pp. 191–92)

Morris Keeton, CAEL's founding president, puts the challenges of objective assessment in a similar context:

> The basis for gaining reliability and validity is the reliance on converging collective judgments of subject-matter experts. There is no such thing as objective judgment. All assessment is subjective. Objective assessments are the convergence of the subjective judgments of qualified assessors who have a minimum of reasons for bias in their judgments.

The Nature of Evidence and Some Key Questions

Evidence suggested and collected in support of the Principles will vary greatly in quantity and quality. At the outset, it may be more important for the team working on the self-assessment worksheets to brainstorm—with little critical reflection—upon the various kinds of evidence that the institution has to demonstrate its observance of the Principles. Next, consider the possibility that some evidence generated in support of one Principle might also apply to another Principle. After spending such energy searching for relevant evidence, the team can undertake a more critical reflection upon the nature of the evidence. The crucial questions will be how much credence and trust should be placed in the evidence offered, as true indicators of the institution's performance.

Here are some valuable questions to consider about the nature of the evidence you will collect:

1. *Validity*—Does the documentation relate directly to the key *Principles of Effectiveness* and Best Practice Performance Indicators that are being assessed?

2. *Sufficiency*—Can the documentation serve as conclusive proof for one or more of the *Principles of Effectiveness* being assessed? What else might be required?

3. *Currency*—Is the documentation relatively recent and up-to-date in relation to the *Principles of Effectiveness* being assessed?

4. *Authenticity*—Is the evidence genuine? Does it give an accurate picture of your institution's performance in relation to the *Principles of Effectiveness* being assessed?

The most difficult question to answer about evidence is, "How representative is this evidence of the typical performance of the institution?" Outstanding practices—performed only irregularly—can hardly give comfort or satisfaction to anyone, especially the students who are the intended beneficiaries. Here again there is no right answer. When completing the worksheets and working with your team, one tactic may be to give the institution the benefit of the doubt—taking credit for demonstrating a best practice, somewhat infrequently—while simultaneously gaining consensus that the issue of quality assurance (consistent performance) is attached. However, if there is no agreement that quality must be improved in such cases, then it is little more than self-deluding to claim that the practices have been successfully implemented.

Now is the time to address the Principles. The chapters that follow may be addressed in any order of your choosing. Good outcomes are possible from doing a few chapters, or even a single chapter. However, we urge you to complete all of the chapters and worksheets. The Principles are comprehensive and integrated, and the best of the Adult Learning Focused Institutions systematically address each of the Principles, not just a few. Unless the full scope of what it means to be an Adult Learning Focused Institution is addressed, then a few good outcomes may not find sufficient ground to take root, grow, and thrive within your college or university. Nor, for that matter, will the adult learners you endeavor to serve.

In Chapter 12 we will provide ideas on how to take stock of your self-assessment activities and how to circumvent the obstacles to building an Adult Learning Focused Institution.

Chapter 4

The Outreach Principle

Principle:

The institution conducts its outreach to adult learners by overcoming barriers of time, place, and tradition in order to create lifelong access to educational opportunities.

"One of my advisees told me that she twice drove into the college parking lot, sat in her car and then drove away before she finally had the nerve to come inside to get program and enrollment information."

—an adult educator

The general public has a traditional view of higher education: 18–23 year old students living in residence on an ivy-covered campus. To convey the message that higher education is available to busy adults requires more aggressive practices than well-placed print materials or direct-mail campaigns. Adult learners are often apprehensive about entering into the college or university environment, so Adult Learning Focused Institutions (ALFIs) utilize a variety of innovative methods and diverse venues to communicate with them about educational programs, support services, and career opportunities.

Recruitment

The adult-focused institution frames its view of higher education in relation to the world beyond its own campus boundaries. It challenges traditional assumptions about higher education in the variety of ways that it attempts to communicate with potential adult students. The ALFI reaches out to adult learners in their communities and workplaces by attending community meetings, and by setting up presentations on-site at various companies and "one-stop," multi-purpose community centers. These are a few of the ways that institutions introduce the benefits, opportunities and challenges of higher education to adults who may be interested in returning to formal study to pursue a variety of personal and career goals. Reframing the theory and practice of higher education outside the traditional framework is one of the many things that an Adult Learning Focused Institution must do.

ALFIs work hard to make the potential adult student's first contact with the institution a welcoming and affirming experience. This can be as simple as making sure that a potential student gets her questions answered in a timely and friendly way. A one-stop center open during non-business hours for information on admission, financial aid, and advising can help adult learners to deal positively with some of the common barriers associated with returning to formal study. Reducing barriers that often intimidate adults and prevent them from pursuing a college degree can greatly diminish their anxiety and enhance their ability to take the risky first steps toward enrolling in a program of study.

Admission

Adults are generally unaccustomed to viewing themselves in the traditional role of student. The staff and faculty at an ALFI work collaboratively with potential students to ensure that they clearly understand the responsibilities and benefits of returning to formal study, the demands that will be made on them personally, and the supports and services offered by the institution to help them achieve their goals. The best retention efforts begin prior to formal admission. The institution communicates with adult learners by initially providing information and counseling to them on their own turf, acknowledging the legitimacy of their family and community responsibilities, recognizing the worth of their previous learning and inviting them to be active partners in the educational planning process. The outreach process, as practiced by ALFIs, makes formal enrollment less of a major hurdle for adults because many of the fears and misgivings usually associated with returning to school are dealt with much earlier in the recruitment process.

> The best retention efforts begin prior to formal admission.

The admissions process begins informally by helping adult students gain a realistic picture of what it means to go to a college or university and by introducing them to the people and services that can help them succeed. This process continues after the adult learner has been formally admitted to the institution, throughout the time spent enrolled in the institution, and often after graduation.

Program Delivery

Outreach means more than customized marketing and recruitment of an older student target market. The ALFI continually examines the ways in which it reaches out and interacts with adult learners. These institutions eagerly gather feedback from students and alumni through surveys and focus groups. ALFIs have to deliver on their promises to provide flexible, collaborative and convenient programs. Therefore, "Outreach" activities also affect current enrollees because they are seen as partners in the design, delivery, and evaluation of curricula, and the ways in which student support is offered. Outreach to adult learners entails addressing their needs in ways that work for them, and that may well mean taking the operations of the admissions office, bookstore, and classroom to the places where adults live and work instead of waiting for adults to come to campus.

Reducing barriers for adult students also means creating new roles for faculty, who are the key contacts for adult learners. These roles can include becoming managers and facilitators of student learning, rather than lecturers, and feeling comfortable learning from students without professional embarrassment. Adult learners can be recognized as potential co-creators of knowledge if their experiences are understood as a means to continually enrich and contribute to the learning process and the culture of the institution, rather than as evidence of a disconnect between academic theory and real life. It is through relationships with supportive faculty that adult learners gain confidence in their student role (Kasworm & Pike, 1994; Blowers & Kasworm, 1994).

The Outreach Principle, then, is a license to innovate, and sets the stage for the other Principles of Effectiveness* for Serving Adult Learners as outlined in this book. Reducing barriers to learners is in keeping with higher education's historic role in crossing boundaries, especially through the creation of new knowledge that supplants ignorance and error, and through the enrichment of the cultural environment through new (and sometimes controversial) forms of expression. This stance against unnecessary barriers and for innovation is also what has placed institutions of higher education in a leadership role within society, reducing the marginalization of women, minorities, and the disenfranchised.

Performance Indicators of This Principle in Action

An Adult Learning Focused Institution:

❖ Uses a variety of innovative methods and venues to recruit adult learners;

❖ Creates recruitment and admissions practices and services that address the personal needs and concerns of adults who are unaccustomed to viewing themselves in the 'traditional' role of a student;

❖ Works collaboratively with adults to help them overcome barriers that may prevent them from returning to learning;

❖ Assists adult learners in making informed decisions about how well the college matches their interests and goals; and

❖ Hires faculty who willingly perform a variety of roles that include advising, teaching, and facilitating and connecting learners to support services.

Best Practices or Examples of Evidence That May Demonstrate This Principle in Action
(see also Appendix B, Page References to the CAEL Benchmarking Study)

❖ Workplace-based recruiting and student support activities;

❖ Clear, jargon-free advertising flyers distributed both on- and off-campus in community centers, libraries, public offices, and workplaces;

❖ Surveys conducted in a variety of formats including telephone, print, and e-mail;

❖ Information requested from adult learners about their learning needs, followed up by personal interviews with faculty and staff at times and locations convenient for the learners;

❖ Orientation and information sessions conducted at key times and locations in which faculty, staff, current learners, and graduates meet with adult learners to discuss their learning needs and to identify necessary supports and resources;

❖ Multiple entry/re-entry points for programs;

❖ Special events such as weekend institutes that enable adult learners to sample the institution's course and program offerings, meet faculty and current students, and sit-in on classes prior to making a final decision about enrolling;

❖ Gathering feedback from adult learners related to course and program evaluations that describe the support and flexibility provided by the institution;

❖ Off-campus or distributed instructional sites/opportunities. For example, providing courses, counseling, admissions, and support services, including day care, in the communities and workplaces in which adult learners live and work;

❖ Modularized curricula or 'block' scheduling of courses;

❖ 'Off hours' (non-daytime) instructional capability; and

❖ Flexible, seminar-style seating in classrooms.

References

Blowers, Sally, S. & Kasworm, Carol E. (1994). *Adult Undergraduate Students: Patterns of Learning Involvement.* Washington, D.C.: Office of Educational Research and Improvement, U.S. Department of Education.

Flint, Thomas A. & Associates. (1999). *Best Practices in Adult Learning: A CAEL/APQC Benchmarking Study.* Dubuque: Kendall-Hunt.

Kasworm, Carol E. & Pike, Gary R. (1994). Adult undergraduate students: Evaluating the appropriateness of a traditional model of academic performance. *Research in Higher Education,* 35 (6), 689-710.

Outreach

Example of the Principle in Action

School of New Resources, College of New Rochelle—New York City

THE ACCESS PROGRAM

Prospective students interested in the School of New Resources (SNR) are invited to come to the campus of their choice (there are seven campuses around New York City) to meet with an advisor on either a one-to-one or small group basis. SNR strongly believes that a live encounter—via telephone or a face-to-face chat—is the most effective method of communication with adult learners. Their motto is "we don't just wait for adults to come to us, we reach out."

Reception staff members are trained to greet adult learners in a friendly, helpful manner and to create a warm, inviting climate for communication. When possible, members of the reception support team are current or former students who can immediately identify with the anxieties experienced by an adult at the prospect of returning to formal study. During the initial contact with the SNR, prospective students receive an overview of the School and they are encouraged to ask questions, discuss their educational and career goals, anxiety, and reasons for returning to school.

SNR makes available a number of services to assist adult learners in deciding whether the School can help them achieve their educational goals.

A key element of the admissions process is the Adult Career Counseling Education and Support Services Program (ACCESS). The program addresses a range of barriers adults may encounter as they seek to enter college, including transportation, child care, financial needs, time management, and budgeting. The ACCESS Program also provides services to address the needs of students who may require additional academic preparation in order to be admitted. These include tutorial services, developmental writing courses, testing opportunities, peer advising and group tutorials.

From the CAEL Benchmarking Study, pp. 55–56 (Flint & Associates, 1999).

Outreach

Example of the Principle in Action

Marylhurst University—Marylhurst, Oregon

SAMPLE MARYLHURST

Marylhurst believes that outreach to prospective adult learners must be based on a communication process that is honest and forthright about what it means to return to university-level studies, including the time commitment.

There is a strong tradition of peer support at Marylhurst. Prospective students are often introduced to the institution by others who have attended the University.

Marylhurst has a program called Sample Marylhurst that enables prospective students to sit in on four to five classes, usually held on Saturdays, prior to making an enrollment decision. Sample Marylhurst enables adult learners to experience first hand how classes are conducted at the university and to engage in dialogue with faculty and learners about the requirements, demands, expectations and benefits of attending Marylhurst. Enrolled adult learners play a significant role in providing interested adults with information about their experiences with the University's programs and services from an adult learner/consumer perspective.

Marylhurst also has an active faculty development committee that is constantly seeking ways to enhance faculty development. The university works intensely with new faculty members to prepare them to work with adult learners in a more facilitative, collaborative, and interactive style both within and outside of the classroom. Adult learners are encouraged by the university to provide feedback to instructors whose approach to teaching and learning is not participatory enough.

From the CAEL Benchmarking Study, p. 54 (Flint & Associates, 1999).

OUTREACH PRINCIPLE ACTIVITY

To evaluate the extent to which your institution is implementing practices that relate to this Principle, you may wish to complete the informal *Institutional Self-Assessment Worksheet* which follows this explanation.

As you work your way through the worksheet pay particular attention to the Best Practices Performance Indicators and use them to help you reflect upon the practices at your own institution. The Performance Indicators on the worksheet are by no means inclusive of all possible indicators. Feel free to add performance indicators not listed on the sheet but used at your institution.

Using the Worksheet

As you look at individual or groups of performance indicators, make decisions about whether or not there is evidence of the Principle in practice at your college or university. The worksheet has a three-step process. First, mark the appropriate column: *Yes (Y), No (N),* or *Under Development (UD)*. Next, write down what person or unit is responsible for making sure that the appropriate practice, process, or procedure happens. Finally, cite the evidence to support your evaluation.

1. **To decide which column to mark (Y, N, or UD), consider these criteria: Is the evidence supporting your decision:**

   a. **Valid?** Does it relate directly to this Principle and the Performance Indicators?

   b. **Sufficient?** Does it show broad and consistent presence in your institution (depending upon how broadly you have defined the "institution" here)?

   c. **Current?** Is it observable today? Will it be observable tomorrow?

   d. **Authentic?** Is it genuine? Is it accurate? Is it sufficiently plentiful to be considered representative of typical institutional practice?

   Tip: Use the "Under Development" column for items whose status is currently unknown, or whose plans are in progress but not yet implemented. Consider these high priority items, the status of which should be revisited by the team quickly.

2. Regardless of how the evidence meets the above criteria, ask: **Who performs—or should perform—the activities or procedures entailed by the Performance Indicators?** Identify the unit(s) or person(s). If those units/persons are not participating in this activity, then they may need to be recruited for purposes of obtaining information needed here, or for implementing an improvement strategy.

3. Cite the evidence that relates to your evaluation in the Y/N/UD columns. Avoid using evidence rooted only in personal, subjective judgement. **What concrete, tangible evidence may others observe to substantiate your decision?**

OUTREACH PRINCIPLE

The institution conducts its outreach to adult learners by overcoming barriers of time, place, and tradition in order to create lifelong access to educational opportunities.

Legend:

Y =   Yes
N =   No
UD =   Under Development

PERFORMANCE INDICATORS	Y	N	UD	UNIT/PERSON RESPONSIBLE	EVIDENCE
Exemplary practice supporting this Principle occurs when an institution:					
• Uses a variety of special methods and venues to recruit adult learners.					
• Has recruitment and admissions practices and services that address the personal needs and concerns of adults who are unaccustomed to viewing themselves in the 'traditional' role of a student.					
• Works collaboratively with adults to help them overcome barriers that may prevent them from returning to learning.					
• Assists adult learners in making informed decisions about how well the college matches their interests and goals.					
• Hires faculty who perform a variety of roles that include advising, teaching, and facilitating and connecting learners to support services.					

See Glossary in Appendix F for Definitions

Chapter 5

The Life and Career Planning Principle

Principle

The institution addresses adult learners' life and career goals before or at the onset of enrollment in order to assess and align its capacities to help learners reach their goals.

As adult experiences are diverse, so too will be the shape and direction of the future that they envision for themselves. Many adult learners have a clear idea of what the end result of their education will be, such as entry into a specific professional career or gaining a promotion. Other adults may be less clear about their goals and look to the education experience for new perspectives and new opportunities. Regardless of their goals, most adults have limited time, money and energy to pursue them. An Adult Learning Focused Institution (ALFI) has an on-going life and career planning structure designed primarily to help adults complete their education as efficiently and effectively as possible in pursuit of their goals.

Before Enrollment

The Adult Learning Focused Institution initiates the process of helping adult learners in life and career planning often before they are formally admitted into the institution. The ALFI focuses on ensuring that it is capable of providing the academic and support services needed by adult students to meet their diverse life and career goals. This includes acknowledging the limitations of the institution, and recognizing that it may not be capable of helping all students achieve their goals. This may also mean that not every adult student must be admitted to a degree program. For an ALFI, the admissions process includes not only reviewing the students' capabilities for doing academic level work appropriate to higher education, but also assessing its own capabilities for providing the education needed to help applicants achieve their goals. Unless there is a match between the capabilities of the student and the capacity of the institution, the institution will refer prospective students to other institutions better suited to meeting those goals.

For example, if an applicant's goal is to become a certified elementary school teacher, an ALFI will only accept such students who are capable of doing postsecondary work and the institution has a program in teacher education. An ALFI without a teacher education program would not admit such a student into a basic liberal arts program without first alerting him to the options at other institutions that may better meet his needs.

During Enrollment

Life and career planning are integral components of the initial phase of the undergraduate program in the ALFI. The planning process starts with assessment of existing skills, knowledge and resources that the adult learner possesses. For most institutions, assessment focuses on academic skills; upon completion of assessment, students are placed in appropriate classes. The Adult Learning Focused Institution goes beyond this initial assessment process to help the adult learner plot a comprehensive plan to graduation. Academic plans may include setting up tutorials or other support needed to achieve competence in certain academic areas. Plans also outline what courses are needed to pass a specific professional licensure exam, and what courses are accepted for transfer at other institutions, or for further post-graduate study. It may also include when and how internships should be established.

Unlike traditional aged students who build their education planning around their earlier school experience, many adult learners construct their undergraduate education around their years of work and life experience. Many learners use this important prior learning to develop future goals. Requiring adult learners to take courses on subjects that they have already mastered serves no real purpose other than to subject them to a needless or insulting delay on the road to new knowledge. Some adult learners may have earned college credit at other institutions and seek to transfer credits into their current program. Prior learning assessment (PLA)* is an integral part of developing a life and career plan, as it allows adult learners to gain credit for learning from a variety of formal and informal sources. Learning that is equated with the level of higher education, yet acquired prior to enrollment can be accepted towards a degree program if it matches the required learning outcomes of the institution. These credits often accelerate an adult's progress towards attaining a degree. The process is also critical to ongoing planning because, once examined with other components, these credits may point to a career or life opportunity that the adult learner may not have previously considered. At this point, an advisor and the adult learner can work together to develop a plan that will take the adult student to the next stage of his or her educational journey.

An ALFI also helps adult learners to develop and follow through in other areas that need careful planning for a successful undergraduate experience. For example, most adults have been out of a formal education setting for an extensive period of time, and many may need assistance in developing study skills or blending their role as students with their other important roles. Therefore, developing a plan on how and when to study is often helpful. Designing such a plan may include assessing learning styles and strategies in order to assist adult learners with effectively completing assignments, even if they are required to work outside of their preferred styles.

Plans may also include helping the adult learner to take a careful look at how pursuing a degree will impact other aspects of their lives. Life planning includes helping the adult learner create strategies for balancing the demands of family, work, and school. For adult learners, learning how to study and planning time to study are just as important as creating a plan to learn algebra in order to become an accountant.

Ongoing Planning

Focusing on student goals is not a one time event that occurs only at the outset of a program of study. Student goals must be a subject of regular conversation between institutional faculty/staff and its students. It is not uncommon for students' goals to change during their programs, so the ongoing planning process helps adult learners adjust their program to meet emerging needs. Conversations with the adult learner often involve continually reviewing and revising goals, making adjustments, and exploring how the institution might help the learner accomplish new goals. Moreover, regular contact between the institution's representatives, peers, and the adult learner provides emotional support and encouragement throughout the program. These relationships are also important to the retention of adult learners in higher education.

Performance Indicators of This Principle in Action

An Adult Learning Focused Institution:

❖ Collaborates with adult learners to develop a systematic process for education and career planning;

❖ Helps adult learners determine their level of educational development upon entry;

❖ Helps adult learners identify career goals and a plan for reaching those goals;

❖ Uses education and career planning as a method of establishing regular contact with adult learners throughout their program;

❖ Encourages adults to become active partners in the planning, delivery, and evaluation of their own learning;

❖ Demonstrates ways in which adult learners can use both formal and informal assessment as the foundation for making educational decisions;

❖ Uses prior learning assessment to help identify life and career goals; and

❖ Creates pathways for adult learners to gain credit for learning from a variety of sources so that learning appropriate to higher education, yet acquired prior to enrollment, can be accepted towards institutional credentials and degrees.

Best Practices or Examples of Evidence That May Demonstrate This Principle in Action
(see also Appendix B, Page References to the CAEL Benchmarking Study)

❖ Course placement process guided by services that assist adults with initial educational planning, assessment of prior learning, and preparation of documentation necessary to have their learning assessed for academic credit;

❖ Course offerings in Life or Educational Planning, or Career Development, that assist adult learners with enhancing self-esteem and engaging in an ongoing process of life/work planning and goal setting;

❖ Customized orientation sessions for adult students;

❖ Re-entry advising on issues of skill levels, time management, and multiple life roles;

❖ Portfolio development course for credit;

❖ Options for obtaining credit for corporate or military educational courses;

❖ Regular "check-ins" and interventions throughout the adult students academic career at a variety of times and locations (e.g. mornings, evenings, weekends, by e-mail, and by telephone) convenient for the learner;

❖ Utilization of mentors and advisors drawn from a variety of community-based organizations and businesses to complement faculty involvement and ensure relevance of the adult learner's program of study to specific occupations/professions; and

❖ Referrals to networks of providers for services outside the institution's scope or mission.

References

Flint, Thomas A. & Associates (1999). *Best Practices in Adult Learning: A CAEL/APQC Benchmarking Study*. Chicago: Council for Adult and Experiential Learning.

Life and Career Planning

Example of the Principle in Action

Marylhurst University—Marylhurst, Oregon

PRE-ENROLLMENT

Marylhurst has a Learning Assessment Center (LAC) designed to assist adult learners with initial educational planning, assessment of prior learning and preparation of necessary documentation to have this learning assessed for academic credit. All new learners are required to take writing and mathematics tests at the LAC to complete the admissions process. Marylhurst also uses self-assessment tools to determine the skill level of adult learners and it offers learning enrichment classes to help learners develop skills and strategies for formal study. Life Planning and Career Development courses are offered which assist adult learners with enhancing self-esteem and engaging in a continuous process of life/work planning and goal setting.

From the CAEL Benchmarking Study, p. 61 (Flint & Associates, 1999)

ONGOING PLANNING

Adult learners are expected to take an active role in the planning and evaluation of their own learning, and collaboration among learners and faculty is encouraged. All degree programs at Marylhurst have a self-design component which usually begins with learners writing their own mission statement. This activity helps to determine the structure and direction of their degree program.

Marylhurst has a set of clearly defined general education learning outcomes for each of its degree programs. These outcomes, coupled with the collaborative approach to educational planning and delivery, make it possible for adult learners to organize their learning around their personal interests and priorities. The development of an Educational Degree Plan is a requirement for all learners. It is created by the adult learner in collaboration with an academic advisor and it outlines all of the core and general educational requirements needed for graduation. Early on in their degree planning sessions learners are encouraged to enter into internships with local employers to enhance their networking opportunities prior to graduation.

From the CAEL Benchmarking Study, p. 62 (Flint & Associates, 1999).

Life and Career Planning

Example of the Principle in Action

DePaul University—Chicago, Illinois

THE SCHOOL FOR NEW LEARNING (SNL)

The School for New Learning (SNL) is conscious of the fact that providing too much information too soon to prospective students can be overwhelming. As a result, its personnel (faculty, staff, professional advisors) work as a team in responding to student queries with accurate, concise information using consistent language to describe the outcomes-based curriculum and the demands of formal study that will be made on the learner's family, work, and community commitments.

The SNL respects the prior learning of adult students and utilizes some of that learning both formally and informally to assist them in designing their educational programs and receiving credit for experiential learning related to the outcomes in the SNL competence framework. The school has a systematic, six-step educational planning process that includes one-on-one advising sessions, workshops, and small group meetings devoted to planning, implementing, and evaluating learning. The six-step process includes:

1. Individual interview (optional).
2. Foundations of Adult Learning course.
3. Initial committee meeting to set program objectives, identify outcomes, and develop a preliminary program plan.
4. Mid-point program meeting to assess progress.
5. Final committee meeting to document and assess completion of learning goals and competency.
6. Summit seminar to reflect on the learning process, share accomplishments, and consider future academic goals.

From the CAEL Benchmarking Study, pp. 63–4 (Flint & Associates, 1999).

LIFE AND CAREER PLANNING PRINCIPLE ACTIVITY

To evaluate the extent to which your institution is implementing practices that relate to this Principle, you may wish to complete the informal *Institutional Self-Assessment Worksheet* which follows this explanation.

As you work your way through the worksheet pay particular attention to the Best Practices Performance Indicators and use them to help you reflect upon the practices at your own institution. The Performance Indicators on the worksheet are by no means inclusive of all possible indicators. Feel free to add performance indicators not listed on the sheet but used at your institution.

Using the Worksheet

As you look at individual or groups of performance indicators, make decisions about whether or not there is evidence of the Principle in practice at your college or university. The worksheet has a three-step process. First, mark the appropriate column: *Yes (Y), No (N)* or *Under Development (UD)*. Next, write down what person or unit is responsible for making sure that the appropriate practice, process or procedure happens. Finally, cite the evidence to support your evaluation.

1. **To decide which column to mark (Y, N, or UD), consider these criteria: Is the evidence supporting your decision:**

   a. **Valid?** Does it relate directly to this Principle and the Performance Indicators?

   b. **Sufficient?** Does it show broad and consistent presence in your institution (depending upon how broadly you have defined the institution here)?

   c. **Current?** Is it observable today? Will it be observable tomorrow?

   d. **Authentic?** Is it genuine? Is it accurate? Is it sufficiently plentiful to be considered representative of typical institutional practice?

   Tip: Use the "Under Development" column for items whose status is currently unknown, or whose plans are in progress but not yet implemented. Consider these high priority items, the status of which should be revisited by the team quickly.

2. Regardless of how the evidence meets the above criteria, ask: **Who performs—or should perform—the activities or procedures entailed by the Performance Indicators?** Identify the unit(s) or person(s). If those units/persons are not participating in this activity, then they may need to be recruited for purposes of obtaining information needed here, or for implementing an improvement strategy.

3. Cite the evidence that relates to your evaluation in the Y/N/UD columns. Avoid using evidence rooted only in personal, subjective judgement. **What concrete, tangible evidence may others observe to substantiate your decision?**

LIFE AND CAREER PLANNING PRINCIPLE

The institution addresses adult learners' life and career goals before or at the onset of enrollment in order to assess and align its capacities to help learners reach their goals.

Legend:

Y = Yes
N = No
UD = Under Development

PERFORMANCE INDICATORS	Y	N	UD	UNIT/PERSON RESPONSIBLE	EVIDENCE
Exemplary practice supporting this Principle occurs when an institution:					
● Collaborates with adult learners to develop a systematic process for education and career planning.					
● Helps adult learners determine their level of educational development upon entry.					
● Helps adult learners identify career goals and a plan for reaching those goals.					
● Uses education and career planning as a method of establishing regular contact with adult learners throughout their program.					
● Encourages adults to become active partners in the planning, delivery, and evaluation of their own learning.					
● Demonstrates ways in which adult learners can use both formal and informal assessment as the foundation for making educational decisions.					
● Uses prior learning assessment to help identify life and career goals.					
● Creates pathways for adult learners to gain credit for learning from a variety of sources so that appropriate learning acquired prior to enrollment can be accepted towards institutional credentials and degrees.					

See Glossary in Appendix F for Definitions

Chapter 6

The Financing Principle

Principle

The institution promotes choice using an array of payment options for adult learners in order to expand equity and financial flexibility.

Money matters—it is no less true for adult students than for younger students. **Money** (in addition to **time**) is one of the most commonly cited barriers to adult enrollment in higher education. Many institutions of higher education study their tuition and financial assistance policies and practices in order to 'leverage' the best possible enrollment outcomes within their student markets. Often, such studies frequently focus upon the traditional aged population, with the intent of targeting financial resources upon that group of students most likely to enroll full time and to use institutional residential facilities—in other words, those students whose direct institutional expenses will be highest. At least two dilemmas ensue for those interested in assisting adult learners. First, it is impossible to derive general principles from the findings of such unrelated studies, because institutional circumstances and methodologies vary so greatly. More specifically, adult decision-making about financial issues may be very different from that of young students and their parents.

Thus, it is unusual to find research such as that done recently for the Australian Vice Chancellors Committee (AVCC), which commissioned a study of their Higher Education Contribution Scheme (HECS) affecting the broad range of Australian colleges and universities. The HECS scheme permits students to pay a percentage of their tuition fees upon matriculation, thereafter receiving the balance of funds as a loan from the federal government. Former students repay their HECS debt following graduation when their salary reaches a specified threshold. Yet, recently the threshold was reduced, effectively increasing the net costs to current and future students, who would be obliged to begin paying their loans much sooner after graduation.

The AVCC study attempted to isolate the effects of HECS policy changes upon 'mature' (non-teenage, defined as age 20–45) students. The impact has been shown to be dramatic. As reported to AVCC, an analysis of interest in higher education by mature students (as reflected by their applications) concluded, "… the analysis indicates that they may have been reduced due to the recent HECS changes. The number of applicants is tentatively estimated to have fallen by *10,000 persons or 10 percent* of mature applicants due to changes announced in 1997" (italics added) (Andrews,1997). The executive director of the Australian Vice-Chancellors Committee, who was quoted for a newspaper story on the topic, remarked,

> The mature-age student population is important if we're going to have a highly skilled workforce. Workers have got to be committed to upgrading their skills

through life rather than just looking at education as something they did when they were young. A decline in mature-age students shows a falling commitment from people to lifelong education, which is a broader economic and social worry for the country. (Owen, 1998)

The AVCC study dramatically exposes the flaws in assumptions commonly held about adult financing of higher education. Often, the general assumption is that adults are more resourceful than younger students; thus, they are assumed to be more 'immune' to the effects of potentially adverse financial policies. One assumption is that for working adults, employers will pay the bill. Privacy concerns for both the students and their employers make accurate measures difficult to obtain, but some data has been estimated on U.S. higher education by the National Center for Education Statistics (NCES)*. These estimates show that during the mid-1990s, employer educational assistance was received by only three percent of all undergraduate students. Even among graduate or professional school students, only seven percent are estimated to receive financial assistance from their employers. Yet, nearly half of all U.S. undergraduates, and nearly all graduate/first professional students, are self-supporting (adult) students for whom parental financial assistance is not expected (Tuma & Geis, 1995).

In the U.S., degree-seeking students are far more likely to have received federal, state, or institutional financial assistance than employer aid. Among those students who are considered to be financially independent of their parents (usually age 24 years or older), approximately 33 percent of those without dependents (children) and approximately 30 percent of those with dependents receive some form of federal student financial assistance. These percentages are roughly comparable to traditional aged student recipients. Approximately one-quarter of independent students demonstrate evidence of financial need that qualifies them for grant assistance, and an estimated twenty percent receive federally-backed student loans to attend institutions of higher education (Tuma & Geis, 1995).

As is true for so many of the practices exemplifying the other Principles of Effectiveness* in the ALFI* framework, the Financing Principle recognizes the importance of the goals of equity and flexibility for adults. By equity we mean that outcomes are fair and just for adults—not that the outcomes invariably must be equal to those for other students. In practice, this means that the special circumstances of adult students should be properly accounted for—rather than simply ignored—within institutional procedures and practices. By flexibility we mean that the solutions that are offered to adult students to address their issues demonstrate the ability of the institution to bend without breaking the rules of good practice. Rules have no value if they become ends in themselves. A flexible institution puts the highest value upon the achievement of goals; accordingly, it recognizes multiple paths toward its goals and eliminates barriers that unreasonably restrict the paths toward them.

> A flexible institution puts the highest value upon the achievement of goals; accordingly, it recognizes multiple paths toward its goals and eliminates barriers that unreasonably restrict the paths toward them.

Achieving Equity

In the first chapter of this book we identified a number of characteristics typical of adult learners, including: delayed enrollment, part-time enrollment, full-time employment, and dependents (including a spouse). In the financial realm, it is somewhat unlikely that the policies and practices of the institution deliberately discriminate against the adult learner on the basis of age alone (if so, consider beginning an open discussion of the express purpose of such rules). Yet, the institution might have policies and practices governing factors such as those just listed which have a disproportionate impact upon adult learners. For example, if the institution has forms of financial assistance available only to first-time (never-before-enrolled) students, then many (if not most) adult learners may not have access to it, because adult learners often spread their attendance out over many years and many institutions. Similarly, if the institution restricts certain forms of financial assistance to only full-time students then, again, many adults will not qualify.

Accordingly, the process of expanding equity for adult learners under this Financing Principle might well begin with an examination of policies and practices that have explicit exclusions, asking first what the goal of such prohibitions may be. Second, a close examination of whatever evidence may be available is in order, showing that the exclusionary policies are factually grounded and capable of delivering the desired outcomes—without any unwanted side effects. Finally, one might ask if the current policies are the only appropriate way to achieve the desired goals, or whether additional options are appropriate.

For example, imagine that an institution excludes part-time students from a financial assistance program, the goal being to allocate limited resources. Although the goal is realistic, assume here that one result is the near-total exclusion of adult recipients within that aid program. One solution might be the development of an approach that qualifies part-time students but appropriately pro-rates the size of the financial award based on the number of courses for which they have enrolled.

Demonstrating Flexibility

Ironically, the small percent of adult students who do receive employer assistance (as mentioned at the opening of this chapter) often find themselves in a financial quandary about using that benefit. In the U.S., many companies have designed their employee tuition assistance programs to pay a variable amount that depends upon the final grades or marks earned by the employee/student. Thus, to obtain the company's funds, the employee/student requests reimbursement in the weeks or months after the course is completed. However, since the standard policy of many U.S. institutions of higher education is that students pay tuition and fees before beginning their studies, some students may be stuck—unless they have sufficient personal funds, or access to some other outside source, they may be unable to start their program, no matter how confident they may be of their eventual academic success.

An Adult Learning Focused Institution (ALFI) will recognize the above dilemma for employed students and will have flexibly adopted its practices to create access. In the example above, several options are possible while awaiting reimbursement from the student's employer:

❖ A short-term loan arranged by the institution (at low or no interest);
❖ The use of revolving credit (such as credit cards);
❖ A billing plan that splits the tuition and fees into segments payable over the academic term rather than the entire balance being due at the outset; or
❖ Special help to adults to secure enough financial aid to pay the first term enrolled.

Performance Indicators of This Principle in Action

An Adult Learning Focused Institution:

❖ Informs adult learners about convenient payment options available to them;
❖ Assists adult learners through deferred payment options when tuition reimbursement programs do not make funds available until course completion;
❖ Makes financial aid and grants available to part-time students;
❖ Assesses charges to learners incrementally during the course of a program and establishes equitable refund policies;

* ❖ Helps learners to develop strategies for locating external funding sources to assist with education costs;
* ❖ Ensures that the learner is not caught between the institution and external tuition assistance sponsors regarding tuition payment issues; and
* ❖ Designs accurate and understandable accounting reports so that billing statements are clear and billing cycles are convenient for the learner or the learner's sponsors.

Best Practices or Examples of Evidence That May Demonstrate This Principle in Action
(see also Appendix B, Page References to the CAEL Benchmarking Study)

* ❖ Pro-rata system for tuition charges and tuition refunds;
* ❖ Deferred payment for students obtaining tuition reimbursement after course completion;
* ❖ Institution-funded financial aid awards (including grants) for part-time and/or adult students;
* ❖ Equitable allocation of donated or government-funded aid to adult learners;
* ❖ 'Off hours' (non-daytime) financial advising and transaction processing;
* ❖ Availability of pre-registration financial aid counseling;
* ❖ Written materials sent to adults describing flexible payment options;
* ❖ Application fee waivers for adult learners having financial hardship;
* ❖ Discounted tuition rates for multiple family members enrolled; and
* ❖ Discounted group rate for adults employed at the same company or sharing a similar affiliation such as union membership.

References

Andrews, Les (1997). *The Effects of the Higher Education Contribution Scheme on Interest in Undertaking Higher Education.* Paper prepared for the Higher Education Division, Department of Employment, Education, Training, and Youth Affairs. Commonwealth of Australia. Australian Government Printing Service, Canberra, Australia. Report published at http://www.deyta.gov.au/highered/hecseffect/hecshes.htm.

Flint, Thomas A. & Associates (1999). *Best Practices in Adult Learning: A CAEL/APQC Benchmarking Study.* Chicago: Council for Adult and Experiential Learning.

Owen, Michael (1998). "Mature-age undergraduate student numbers in South Australian universities are falling, prompting a warning that the decline has serious implications for the State's workforce," in the *Sunday Mail* (South Australia), Sunday, May 3, 1998.

Tuma, John and Geis, Sonya (1995). *Student Financing of Undergraduate Education, 1992–93.* NCES Report 95-202. Washington, DC: National Center for Education Statistics. U.S. Department of Education.

The Financing Principle

Example of the Principle in Action

Syracuse University—Syracuse, New York

CONTINUING EDUCATION DIVISION

The Continuing Education Division of Syracuse University (SU), established in 1920, has long sought to create a series of strategies that enable adult students to view the University's education as affordable. The strategies cover a gamut from tuition rates to financial aid to billing practices:

1. The Division deliberately sets a tuition rate for part-time students lower than a proportionately reduced full-time rate.
2. SU has established a deferred payment option, requiring 20 percent payment down at enrollment with the balance due in 45 days. A provision for using credit cards enables students to extend this time.
3. An Employer Deferred Payment plan was created in the early 1990s to allow employed students to defer their tuition payment until the following semester, provided that the student signs a promissory note and documents his or her eligibility for the employers' tuition reimbursement plans.
4. Adult students lacking an employer tuition reimbursement plan are offered a monthly installment option for paying their tuition bills.
5. Higher Education Opportunity Program (HEOP) grants. SU created this program in the 1970's to create access for adults who are disadvantaged financially. The program began with institutional funds only, but proved so innovative that eventually public funding from the state extended to numerous institutions.
6. The Incentive Grant program is for new part-time undergraduates and for students returning after an absence of at least five years. Upon fulfilling some academic requirements (9–15 credits earned, grade point average of 2.0 or higher, two semesters completed), eligible students obtain 2.25 to 4.5 units of instructional credits free of charge in their third and fourth semesters.
7. SU creates access for adults transferring from other institutions into part-time study at SU through its Achiever Scholarship. For this award, incoming transfer students must have at least a 'B' grade average and 30 units of transferable course work. If they maintain high grades at SU, they continue to receive the grant, effectively reducing their tuition fee by 25 to 35 percent for 90 units, six years, or until graduation.

Kristensen, Linda G. (2002). Financial solutions give part-time students access to higher education. *CAEL Forum & News*, 25 (2), 26-27.

The Financing Principle

Example of the Principle in Action

DePaul University—Chicago, Illinois

SCHOOL FOR NEW LEARNING

A competency-based degree program for adults such as that of the School for New Learning at DePaul University poses unique financing issues. Nonetheless, most students in the program must still contend with tuition charges and, like many other adult-serving programs, the School for New Learning draws many students who work for area employers. Since many employed adults participate in tuition reimbursement plans from their employers, the School must deal with the situation in which students must successfully complete academic work—and provide proof of payment—before the employer's reimbursement is issued. All too often this puts students at other colleges and universities—especially lower-income students—in an impossible situation: they have the ability to succeed but not the means, as they are tantalized by funds arriving in the future, and at the same time obliged to use personal funds they do not have. SNL has addressed this problem by creating a program called "DePepper" which permits students to pay only a $100 fee at the time of class registration, deferring the remaining amounts until the course is completed and reimbursement received. Students without employer assistance are permitted to split the total payment into more convenient monthly amounts over the period of enrollment.

In recent years, the School has substantially increased its scholarship opportunities for adults. The School has five different financial aid programs available during the school year to help support students. Grants from this program have recently ranged from $1,000 to $2,000.

From the CAEL Benchmarking Study, p. 98 (Flint & Associates, 1999).

FINANCING PRINCIPLE ACTIVITY

To evaluate the extent to which your institution is implementing practices relating to this Principle, you may wish to complete the informal *Institutional Self-Assessment Worksheet* which follows this explanation.

As you work your way through the worksheet pay particular attention to the Best Practices Performance Indicators and use them to help you reflect upon the practices at your own institution. The Performance Indicators on the worksheet are by no means inclusive of all possible indicators. Feel free to add performance indicators not listed on the sheet but used at your institution.

Using the Worksheet

As you look at individual or groups of performance indicators, make decisions about whether or not there is evidence of the Principle in practice at your college or university. The worksheet has a three-step process. First, mark the appropriate column: *Yes (Y), No (N),* or *Under Development (UN).* Next, write down what person or unit is responsible for making sure that the appropriate practice, process or procedure happens. Finally, cite the evidence to support your evaluation.

1. **To decide which column to mark (Y, N, or UD), consider these criteria: Is the evidence supporting your decision:**

   a. **Valid?** Does it relate directly to this Principle and the Performance Indicators?

   b. **Sufficient?** Does it show broad and consistent presence in your institution (depending upon how broadly you have defined the "institution" here)?

   c. **Current?** Is it observable today? Will it be observable tomorrow?

   d. **Authentic?** Is it genuine? Is it accurate? Is it sufficiently plentiful to be considered representative of typical institutional practice?

   Tip: Use the "Under Development" column for items whose status is currently unknown, or whose plans are in progress but not yet implemented. Consider these high priority items, the status of which should be revisited by the team quickly.

2. Regardless of how the evidence meets the above criteria, ask: **Who performs—or should perform—the activities or procedures entailed by the Performance Indicators?** Identify the unit(s) or person(s). If those units/persons are not participating in this activity, then they may need to be recruited for purposes of obtaining information needed here, or for implementing an improvement strategy.

3. Cite the evidence that relates to your evaluation in the Y/N/UD columns. Avoid using evidence rooted only in personal, subjective judgement. **What concrete, tangible evidence may others observe to substantiate your decision?**

FINANCING PRINCIPLE

The institution promotes choice using an array of payment options for adult learners in order to expand equity and financial flexibility.

Legend:

Y =	Yes
N =	No
UD =	Under Development

PERFORMANCE INDICATORS	Y	N	UD	UNIT/PERSON RESPONSIBLE	EVIDENCE
Exemplary practice supporting this Principle occurs when an institution:					
● Provides flexible payment options that fit the individual needs/circumstances of the adult learner.					
● Informs adult learners about convenient payment options.					
● Provides deferred payment options when tuition reimbursement programs do not make funds available until course completion.					
● Identifies financial aid options available for both part-time and returning adult learners.					
● Administers charges to learners incrementally over the duration of a program.					
● Establishes equitable refund policies based on the percentage of course/program completion.					
● Identifies external funding sources that assist adult learners.					
● Has a financial aid policy that allocates awards to the adult student population in proportion to their enrollment.					

See Glossary in Appendix F for Definitions

Chapter 7

The Assessment of Learning Outcomes Principle

Principle

The institution defines and assesses the knowledge, skills, and competencies acquired by adult learners both from the curriculum and from life/work experience in order to assign credit and confer degrees with rigor.

What should a college or university graduate know and be able to do? The issue of learning outcomes and their successful demonstration lies at the heart of widespread calls for accountability. Critics of higher education complain that many of its graduates are not equipped to enter the world of work. And most would agree that the accumulation of passing grades next to course listings on transcripts is unacceptable if learners have not acquired the knowledge, skills, and attitudes to make them effective in the multiple spheres of life including work, family, and community.

Through standards derived from long-standing traditions, colleges and universities have articulated ideals of college-level learning defined across several domains, such as:

❖ Communication (reading, writing, speaking, listening);
❖ Computation (quantitative and scientific reasoning);
❖ Critical thinking (independent judgment, weighing values);
❖ Aesthetic and ethical awareness (appreciation of arts and culture); and
❖ Lifelong learning ('learning to learn' or continuous education).

These domains prescribe a necessary, but by no means sufficient, view of the capabilities that an educated person must have today. To function successfully as parents, employees, and citizens, college-educated people are increasingly called upon to demonstrate their abilities and achievements in the 'soft' skills as much as the 'hard' courses. These include problem-solving, interpersonal diagnosis, teamwork, self-control, and planning among many others.

But how do we know that students have achieved this knowledge and these skills and abilities? Many point to the assessment of learning outcomes as a way to help students learn, to help faculty improve teaching and planning, to develop cohesive curricula, and to make publicly explicit the goals and outcomes of a college education. Tom Angelo describes assessment in part as:

[A]n ongoing process aimed at understanding and improving student learning. It involves making our expectations explicit and public; setting appropriate criteria and high standards for learning quality; systematically gathering, analyzing, and interpreting evidence to determine how well performance matches those expectations and standards; and using the resulting information to document, explain, and improve performance.

(Angelo, 1995, p. 7)

Educational Planning

Assessment of learning outcomes is particularly valuable for adult learners* because most of them have particular education and career goals they wish to reach. Assessment of learning can be connected to knowledge and skills that help adult learners reach these goals. For example, instead of simply learning about the principles of accounting, students may learn how to apply accounting principles to actual accounting procedures and problems. On-going assessment shows adult learners their progress, where they may need additional learning, and how their learning will impact their future goals. Learning outcomes offer a way for adult learners to better articulate and demonstrate their learning to employers.

Fostering Curricular Cohesion and Focusing Instructional Efforts

Assessment of learning outcomes also allows instructors to track the learning progress of their students. In contrast to periodic examinations, effective assessment is continuous. This allows both the professor and student to be aware of the learning process and to pinpoint problem areas. It lowers the chance of a student becoming lost in a course or of a professor covering material the students already know.

Assessment of learning outcomes also assists the curriculum planning process. When faculty are able to articulate what a graduate of their institution should know and be able to do, they then can craft a curriculum that includes assessments of learning to meet these goals. For example, ıe categories of knowledge and skill listed at the beginning of this chapter can be woven ough all class requirements (problem-solving, teamwork, self-reflection, critical thinking, etc.), ile others can be met through particular disciplines (communication, computation, aesthetic l ethical awareness).

Relationship to Secondary and Graduate Education

Adult Learning Focused Institutions (ALFI)* place the undergraduate program in relation to secondary and graduate education. Because most adults entering college have been away from an academic setting for some time, one challenge that colleges and universities face is ensuring that new students are able to do college level work. Assessment of learning outcomes can be used before students ever take a class to ensure that they have the skills and knowledge to succeed. Accurate assessment before students begin classes allows institutions to create effective interventions that address barriers to success. For those who wish to pursue advance degrees good assessment of learning outcomes will concretely show what a student knows and how he or she is able to perform academically.

Recognition of Prior Learning (or Prior Learning Assessment)

Last but not least, clarity about learning outcomes is a pre-requisite for quality assurance in programs recognizing prior learning assessment (PLA), which are vitally important to adult learners. Recognition of prior learning refers to any knowledge building or skills attainment that occurs prior to enrollment or outside of enrollment at a postsecondary institution, assessed for the purpose of awarding college credit.

This practice is important because adult learners have little tolerance and time for taking courses on subjects they have already mastered. Recognizing prior learning allows them to move forward with their education and concentrate on new arenas of learning. It creates pathways for adult learners to gain credit for learning from a variety of sources. It also allows the assessment process to be individualized and flexible enough to accommodate a variety of interests. However, it should be noted that recognition of prior learning is focused on *learning*, not simply on *experience*. For example, working with young children may be an important experience, but it is not possible to receive credit for a course in childhood development unless the appropriate level of learning was gained through this experience.

The Adult Learning Focused Institution gives learners the tools and information they need to achieve expected learning outcomes. It is the institution's responsibility to constantly assess its ability to support the achievement of learning outcomes through its policies, procedures, and services.

Performance Indicators of This Principle in Action

An Adult Learning Focused Institution:

- ❖ Encourages adult learners to take an active role in the assessment process;
- ❖ Designs educational experiences using learning outcomes;
- ❖ Utilizes a variety of valid and reliable assessment techniques to measure learning outcomes;
- ❖ Identifies and documents what learners know and can do as a result of their educational experiences;
- ❖ Evaluates external instructional programs to ensure relevance and rigor for the purpose of granting credit;
- ❖ Advocates for adult learners to gain credit for formal learning achieved via instructional programs delivered by businesses, labor unions, and community based organizations;
- ❖ Communicates actively with stakeholders to identify the knowledge, skills, and abilities they need; and
- ❖ Integrates the perspectives of a range of stakeholders such as businesses and the community in defining learning outcomes.

Best Practices or Examples of Evidence That May Demonstrate This Principle in Action
(see also Appendix B, Page References to the CAEL Benchmarking Study)

- ❖ Competency-based curricula structure.
- ❖ Course syllabi that clearly state learning outcomes and assessment criteria.
- ❖ Multiple techniques used to assess student learning.
- ❖ Resource allocation and training for faculty in writing learning outcomes, multiple assessment techniques, and their application in course work.
- ❖ Curricula that integrates work or industry-based skill standards.

- ❖ Provision for individualized assessment of experiential learning such as PLA, portfolio assisted assessment, challenge and military exams.
- ❖ Learning outcomes for graduates that have institution-wide acceptance and applicability.
- ❖ Practices by which student assessments are integrated into the institutional assessment on student learning.

References

Angelo, Thomas A. (1995) *American Association of Higher Education Bulletin*, Washington, D.C.: American Association of Higher Education, p. 7.

Flint, Thomas A. and Associates (1999). *Best Practices in Adult Learning: A CAEL/APQC Benchmarking Study.* Chicago: Council for Adult and Experiential Learning.

Assessment of Learning Outcomes

Examples of the Principle in Action

DePaul University—Chicago, Illinois
School for New Learning (SNL)

THE COMPETENCY-BASED CURRICULUM

All courses at SNL are based on the achievement of competencies. Competence is defined as "the ability to apply knowledge."[1] Competency statements are categorized within five areas: lifelong learning, arts and ideas, the human community, the scientific world, and a focus area that is defined by the learners' personal goals. To complete a degree a student must demonstrate 50 competencies arranged in a coherent design called the competence framework.

Courses require students to reflect on their experience and bring their insights to bear on what they are learning. For example, a course on the life and work of African-American writer Zora Neale Hurston provides an opportunity to demonstrate the competence, "[The student] can express the values of another culture through its language, arts or customs."[2] In this course, students investigate the "history and perspectives of the African American in the U.S. to identify and analyze key events that influenced the choices that Hurston and others have made."[3] The competence is demonstrated in part by "explaining why particular events...occurred when they did, or why different circumstances are likely to result in particular outcomes."

Notes:
1. BA Program Guide, p. 7. School for New Learning, DePaul University, Chicago, IL.
2. "Their Eyes Were Watching God: The Life and Work of Zora Neale Hurston" A class taught by Deborah W. Holton, Ph.D., Spring 2000, DePaul School for New Learning.
3. Ibid.

Assessment of Learning Outcomes

Examples of the Principle in Action

Sinclair Community College—Dayton, Ohio

EMPLOYABILITY GUARANTEE

All degree programs have clearly defined learning outcomes that demonstrate levels of competence. Specific courses are identified which prepare students for each learning outcome. Courses in vocational programs are closely tied to industry standards and the competencies were established with the assistance of professional bodies, advisory committees and employers. Sinclair's "Guarantee for Job Competency" offers graduates of the Applied Science degree up to nine tuition-free credit hours of additional education if their employers judge them to be lacking in the job skills that are identified by the program's learning outcomes.

CAEL Benchmarking Study, p. 79 (Flint & Associates, 1999).

ASSESSMENT OF LEARNING OUTCOMES PRINCIPLE ACTIVITY

To evaluate the extent to which your institution is implementing practices relating to this Principle, you may wish to complete the informal *Institutional Self-Assessment Worksheet* which follows this explanation.

As you work your way through the worksheet pay particular attention to the Best Practices Performance Indicators and use them to help you reflect upon the practices at your own institution. The Performance Indicators on the worksheet are by no means inclusive of all possible indicators. Feel free to add performance indicators not listed on the sheet but used at your institution.

Using the Worksheet

As you look at individual or groups of performance indicators, make decisions about whether or not there is evidence of the Principle in practice at your college or university. The worksheet has a three-step process. First, mark the appropriate column: *Yes (Y), No (N), Under Development (UD)*. Next, write down what person or unit is responsible for making sure that the appropriate practice, process or procedure happens. Finally, cite the evidence to support your evaluation.

1. **To decide which column to mark (Y, N, or UD), consider these criteria: Is the evidence supporting your decision:**

    a. **Valid?** Does it relate directly to this Principle and the Performance Indicators?

    b. **Sufficient?** Does it show broad and consistent presence in your institution (depending upon how broadly you have defined the "institution" here)?

    c. **Current?** Is it observable today? Will it be observable tomorrow?

    d. **Authentic?** Is it genuine? Is it accurate? Is it sufficiently plentiful to be considered representative of typical institutional practice?

    Tip: Use the "Under Development" column for items whose status is currently unknown, or whose plans are in progress but not yet implemented. Consider these high priority items, the status of which should be revisited by the team quickly.

2. Regardless of how the evidence meets the above criteria, ask: **Who performs—or should perform—the activities or procedures entailed by the Performance Indicators?** Identify the unit(s) or person(s). If those units/persons are not participating in this activity, then they may need to be recruited for purposes of obtaining information needed here, or for implementing an improvement strategy.

3. Cite the evidence that relates to your evaluation in the Y/N/UD columns. Avoid using evidence rooted only in personal, subjective judgement. **What concrete, tangible evidence may others observe to substantiate your decision?**

ASSESSMENT OF LEARNING OUTCOMES PRINCIPLE

The institution defines and assesses the knowledge, skills, and competencies acquired by adult learners both from the curriculum and from life/work experience in order to assign credit and confer degrees with rigor.

Legend:

Y = Yes
N = No
UD = Under Development

PERFORMANCE INDICATORS	Y	N	UD	UNIT/PERSON RESPONSIBLE	EVIDENCE
Exemplary practice supporting this Principle occurs when an institution:					
● Encourages adult learners to take an active role in the assessment process.					
● Designs educational experiences using learning outcomes.					
● Utilizes a variety of valid and reliable assessment techniques to measure learning outcomes.					
● Identifies and documents what learners know and can do as a result of their educational experiences.					
● Evaluates external instructional programs to ensure relevance and rigor for the purpose of granting credit.					
● Advocates for adult learners to gain formal credit for learning achieved via instructional programs delivered by businesses, labor unions, and community based organizations.					
● Communicates actively with stakeholders to identify the knowledge, skills, and abilities they need.					
● Integrates the perspectives of a range of stakeholders such as businesses and the community in defining learning outcomes.					

Chapter 8

The Teaching-Learning Process Principle

Principle

The institution's faculty uses multiple methods of instruction (including experiential and problem-based methods) for adult learners in order to connect curricular concepts to useful knowledge and skills.

The renowned experiential educator John Dewey is quoted as saying, "[People] built bridges before there was a science of bridge-building." Dewey reminds us that drawing on our experience and connecting theory with practice are at the root of effective teaching and learning.

Learning That Connects with Life Experience

Adult learners want their learning to connect with their daily life and work. They want an education that focuses on knowledge and skills they need to succeed in today's society. Therefore it is important that learning approaches at the Adult Learning Focused Institution (ALFI) are built on experience and practice and are pursued as a means to a practical end. The end is translated differently by each individual student according to his or her education and career goals.

Learning that gives adult learners a theoretical framework to use in their daily life and work is an effective way of meeting the needs of the wide range of backgrounds, learning styles, and goals adults bring to higher education. Patricia Cross notes that it is important for workers and citizens in the 21st century to be able to "use their experience to enhance learning and their learning to enrich application." She goes on to note that employers need workers who can think and analyze problems on the job:

> Today, there are so many different jobs, and they change so rapidly, that training for specific jobs has become largely irrelevant. Employers want workers who can think, analyze problems, critique solutions, and perhaps most importantly continue to learn to do their jobs better. That will require the ability to learn from experience, to constantly reflect on what has been learned, to experiment with alternatives, and to evaluate the outcomes.

(Cross, 1999, p. 20–21)

Since most adults pursuing an education are either in the workforce or aspire to enter it, the Adult Learning Focused Institution recognizes that an effective teaching-learning process for adults delivers the curriculum through the voice of experience and reflection as readily as through the voice of the faculty members.

Learning Styles

The typical teaching methods in Western culture utilize kinesthetic learning for children in kindergarten to third grade. From grades four through eight, methods lean towards visual learning. From grades nine and above—including non-academic and business learning environments as well—information is presented through auditory learning methods, such as lectures. But not all adults learn in the same way. Most people have a dominant preference for one of the three methods of learning (Clark, 2000).

Accommodating different learning styles is critical for teaching the adult learner because they are often fearful of entering or re-entering a formal learning setting after many years. Past failures in formal schooling can add to this fear and contribute to high attrition rates. For adults, early success is an important component in helping them stay in the program. Discerning an adult learner's preferred learning mode and providing ways for him or her to work in that mode is a first step in building a foundation for accomplishment. Becoming aware of learning style and then building learning opportunities around that style helps adult learners manage their own learning by giving them tools to reflect on the learning process.

Faculty

The role of the instructor or faculty member is particularly important for the many adult learners who bring a wealth of experience and expertise to the learning process. Faculty members at Adult Learning Focused Institutions do not see adult learners as empty vessels waiting to be filled with information.   Instead they take into account the background, experience and knowledge adults bring to their education and help learners build upon that experience. Faculty members create ways for students to learn from one another, and they embrace the opportunity to learn from their students as well. It is not unusual for a professor to find herself in a situation where an adult student knows more about a particular subject than she does. At an Adult Learning Focused Institution, such a professor is not intimidated by this situation, but uses the student's knowledge as an opportunity to enhance the learning experience.

The Adult Learning Focused Institution also includes professionals from the community who often serve as teachers and mentors. When adult learners can draw on the expertise of those in businesses, professions, societies, and community-based organizations, they can better target their learning to include knowledge and skills they need to succeed in a new career.

Performance Indicators of This Principle in Action

An Adult Learning Focused Institution:

❖ Employs a teaching-learning process that includes a high degree of interaction among learners and between learners and faculty;

❖ Considers adult learners to be co-creators of knowledge. Learning experiences and projects are often designed in cooperation with learners and directly relate to the adult learner's work and personal world;

❖ Offers multiple methods of instructional delivery to enhance convenient access to education and to provide choices to accommodate preferred learning modes;

❖ Uses assessment as an integral part of the learning process and in ways that enhance competency and self-confidence;

❖ Encourages faculty to build upon the knowledge, interests, and life-situations that adults bring to their education to develop learning experiences. When working in partnership with businesses and/or unions, faculty members strive to present material in a framework that incorporates the issues and language of the learners' workplaces and communities; and

❖ Supports full-time faculty's work with adult learners, staff, adjunct faculty, and local community resources to develop collaborative learning experiences.

Best Practices or Examples of Evidence That May Demonstrate This Principle in Action
(see also Appendix B, Page References to the CAEL Benchmarking Study)

❖ Student-led learning opportunities;

❖ Course-level structures having experiential learning for credit (such as cooperative education, field study semesters, internships, or externships);

❖ Course-embedded experiential learning (such as 'problem-based,' 'activity-based,' 'collaborative' and/or 'service' learning);

❖ Individualized or interdisciplinary degree program options;

❖ Student-organized courses or seminars for credit;

❖ Faculty training related to adult learning theory and diverse learning styles;

❖ Narrative academic transcripts; and

❖ Guest lecturing by practitioners.

References

Clark, Don. (2000) www.nwlink.com/~donclark/hrd/sat4.html#learn style.

Cross, Patricia. (1999) *The Cross Papers No. 3.* Mission Viejo: League for Innovation in the Community College and Educational Testing Service.

Flint, Thomas A. and Associates. (1999). *Best Practices in Adult Learning: A CAEL/APQC Benchmarking Study.* Chicago: Council for Adult and Experiential Learning.

The Teaching-Learning Process

Example of the Principle in Action

College of New Rochelle, School of New Resources—New York City area

THE LIFE ARTS PROJECT

The Life Arts Project is a part of all seminars at the School for New Resources. The seminars are interdisciplinary and the project presents students with an opportunity to take the content of the seminar and develop a project of their own interest. Students begin by submitting a proposal that requires them to define learning objectives and the learning methods and modes of assessment they plan to use. The professor must approve the plan.

Projects involve activities that draw on past experiences, and the learning derived from these experiences, with knowledge from the seminar's subject matter. Life Arts Projects often relate to students' community, family, or work life. For example, as part of her Life Arts Project for a seminar in the biological sciences, one student traced the history of sickle cell anemia in her family. For a seminar on social science a student—who was also an employee of a local phone company—conducted and analyzed a survey on African-American employee retention in the company.

The Life Arts Project is presented to all members of the seminar as well as recorded through written documentation. The project may involve a variety of exercises including interviews, research papers, artistic projects, and simulations.

From the CAEL Benchmarking Study, p. 75 (Flint & Associates, 1999).

The Teaching-Learning Process

Example of the Principle in Action

National-Louis University—Chicago, Illinois
Applied Behavioral Science Program

CURRICULUM INTEGRATION

The Applied Behavioral Science program at National-Louis University is based on an adult learning cohort model and is designed to integrate theory and practice throughout the curriculum. A full-time faculty member is assigned to each cohort and serves as an Academic Coordinator. The Academic Coordinator works with the students in a mentoring role throughout the program to help them integrate and transfer their learning to the workplace, as well as personal and other professional settings.

The program emphasizes the "practitioner model"—applying and testing course concepts through interactions with others, in small groups and organizational settings. At the outset of the program students learn to tap one another's experience and background as resources for their coursework. Students bring real-life examples that are used as catalysts for examining behavioral theory. Students are then introduced to temperament types and learning styles. This information is used to help students reflect on their own and others' learning as well as how learning is utilized in behavioral science.

The final component in the program is the "Senior Seminar." In this Seminar students reflect upon the program sequence, integrating common threads running throughout the curriculum. Tools, concepts, human interaction and theoretical background are woven together so that students graduate with the ability to diagnose and understand behavioral dynamics and intervene effectively in the problem-solving and decision-making process.

Frey, Ruth. Interview with William Owens, Assistant Professor, National Louis University.

A Story about Teaching-Learning

Through experiential learning, students become co-creators of knowledge. Some might ask, "How can that be?" Many college and university faculty struggle for years to advance their disciplines. A true story about three people—Noel Swerdlow, Robert Garisto, and Sir Isaac Newton—may illuminate this point.

Robert Garisto was an undergraduate who took five years to obtain a bachelor's degree from the University of Chicago because he was working up to 40 hours per week washing dishes and doing odd jobs to pay his tuition. Sir Isaac Newton needs no introduction. As inventor of calculus and discoverer of the laws of gravity and optics, Newton can rightly be regarded as a super-genius of science. Yet, Garisto took Newton down one notch by discovering an error in the genius' work. Garisto resolved a discrepancy in one of Newton's proofs in *Principia Mathematica* whose origin had eluded scholars for more than 300 years. Garisto's discovery rightly earned him the University's prize for excellence in science—no small feat in an institution whose physics department counts 18 Nobel Prize winners among past or current students and faculty! In fact, at 23 years of age, Garisto had even less life experience than the average adult student.

Who, then, is Noel Swerdlow? He is the professor of astronomy who made the assignment to his students (including Garisto) to work on Newton's proofs. Consider what everyone gained by Swerdlow having asked his students to work on a genuine problem and unsolved mystery. Consider the advance made to the history of physics, the excitement and enthusiasm of Garisto and his peers, and the recognition for the university. Most importantly, consider what Swerdlow's peers—at his university or any other—can glean from this story concerning the teaching-learning process.

Higher education has long favored theory over practice. Yet "practical" problems are rich in educational value. All sorts of practical problems are found in abundance in "the real world"— that is, outside of colleges and universities. Most adult learners approach higher education with many of these genuine problems in mind and are eager to see how their learning from the classroom can be applied to problems that they face every day. How does your institution respond to their concerns?

Notes:
- "After 3 Centuries, a Student Figures That Newton Erred" *New York Times*, June 11, 1987.
- "Isaac Newton Goofed, and It Took Student Robert Garisto to Get to the Core of the Matter" *People Magazine*, June 29, 1987, p. 43.
- "New Superhero at Sigma Xi" *Time Magazine*, June 22, 1987, p. 77.
- "Student Finds Error in Newton's 300-Year-Old Classic Work" *Chronicle of Higher Education*, June 17, 1987, p. 9.

TEACHING-LEARNING PROCESS PRINCIPLE ACTIVITY

To evaluate the extent to which your institution is implementing practices relating to this Principle, you may wish to complete the informal *Institutional Self-Assessment Worksheet* which follows this explanation.

As you work your way through the worksheet pay particular attention to the Best Practices Performance Indicators and use them to help you reflect upon the practices at your own institution. The Performance Indicators on the worksheet are by no means inclusive of all possible indicators. Feel free to add performance indicators not listed on the sheet but used at your institution.

Using the Worksheet

As you look at individual or groups of performance indicators, make decisions about whether or not there is evidence of the Principle in practice at your college or university. The worksheet has a three-step process. First, mark the appropriate column: *Yes (Y), No (N), Under Development (UD)*. Next, write down what person or unit is responsible for making sure that the appropriate practice, process or procedure happens. Finally, cite the evidence to support your evaluation.

1. **To decide which column to mark (Y, N, or UD), consider these criteria: Is the evidence supporting your decision:**

   a. **Valid?** Does it relate directly to this Principle and the Performance Indicators?

   b. **Sufficient?** Does it show broad and consistent presence in your institution (depending upon how broadly you have defined the "institution" here)?

   c. **Current?** Is it observable today? Will it be observable tomorrow?

   d. **Authentic?** Is it genuine? Is it accurate? Is it sufficiently plentiful to be considered representative of typical institutional practice?

   Tip: Use the "Under Development" column for items whose status is currently unknown, or whose plans are in progress but not yet implemented. Consider these high priority items, the status of which should be revisited by the team quickly.

2. Regardless of how the evidence meets the above criteria, ask: **Who performs—or should perform—the activities or procedures entailed by the Performance Indicators?** Identify the unit(s) or person(s). If those units/persons are not participating in this activity, then they may need to be recruited for purposes of obtaining information needed here, or for implementing an improvement strategy.

3. Cite the evidence that relates to your evaluation in the Y/N/UD columns. Avoid using evidence rooted only in personal, subjective judgement. **What concrete, tangible evidence may others observe to substantiate your decision?**

TEACHING-LEARNING PROCESS PRINCIPLE

The institution's faculty use multiple methods of instruction (including experiential and problem-based methods) for adult learners in order to connect curricular concepts to useful knowledge and skills.

Legend:
Y = Yes
N = No
UD = Under Development

PERFORMANCE INDICATORS	Y	N	UD	UNIT/PERSON RESPONSIBLE	EVIDENCE
Exemplary practice supporting this Principle occurs when an institution:					
• Utilizes a teaching/learning process that includes a high degree of interaction among learners, faculty, and the community.					
• Recognizes adult learners as co-creators of knowledge.					
• Collaboratively designs learning experiences and projects directly related to the adult learner's work and personal world.					
• Uses multiple methods of instructional delivery to provide access to education.					
• Uses multiple methods of instructional delivery to accommodate various learning styles.					
• Uses assessment as an integral part of the learning process.					
• Uses a variety of assessment tools.					
• Has faculty integrate adults' knowledge, skills, interests, and life-situations into the curriculum.					
• Has faculty members who incorporate the issues, symbols and language of learners, workplaces, and communities.					
• Develops curricula in partnership with businesses, labor unions, and communities.					
• Supports full-time faculty who work collaboratively with adult learners, adjunct faculty and local community resources to develop learning experiences.					
• Provides, or supports financially, professional development for faculty on effective methods for teaching adults.					

See Glossary in Appendix F for Definitions

Chapter 9

The Student Support Systems Principle

Principle

The institution assists adult learners using comprehensive academic and student support systems in order to enhance students' capacities to become self-directed, lifelong learners.

Although an increasing number of educators have come to recognize the important role that support services play in the lives of adult learners, the misconception persists that adult learners are self-supporting and do not need the same level of support as 18–23 year olds. The reality for many adults is often quite the reverse. They need as much quality academic counseling and support as younger learners, especially in the early stages of their involvement with the institution. There are also some fundamental differences in the nature of the assistance they require.

For example, whereas younger students often have the time and inclination to develop relationships with their classmates, older students often view their education as one of many important tasks to complete during a busy day. Obligations to family, work and general life maintenance crowd the adult learner's schedule, often making it difficult for them to prioritize tasks. When something goes wrong or requires extra time in any of these spheres—a sick child, overtime at work, a glitch in registering for a class—their complex juggling act can be thrown off. An Adult Learning Focused Institution understands that these competing forces are a legitimate part of most adult learners' lives and it provides systems and practices that support the adult so that all the responsibilities can be balanced successfully. Convenience and connection are the two critical elements of developing student support services for working adults.

Convenience

Adults have little time to take care of tasks such as registering for classes, paying tuition, buying books or working out a schedule problem. A strong student services system makes these and other tasks virtually effortless. Many institutions create ways for students to take care of basic administrative tasks online or by phone. For more complex problems, some institutions have developed a call center or dedicated a staff member to act as a liaison with other offices to work out problems for a student. Because adult learners often are trying to fulfill the needs of several people at once, on-site childcare, food service, and convenient transportation can make the difference between making or missing a class.

Connection

A positive human connection is an essential part of the education process. Without it, adult students are likely to become disaffected and drop out, no matter how technically excellent the program may be. If an institution aspires to be Adult Learning Focused, it must devise ways to successfully reach out to its learners.

Helping adult learners connect with others on campus can be accomplished in a number of ways. One successful practice is through systems of mentoring and/or student cohort groups. With mentoring, adult learners establish a trusting, long-term relationship with a person of accomplishment and who has mastered the discipline they are to enter—a person who may or may not be a faculty representative (though preferably should be). Colleges and universities with very large enrollments, well beyond the ability of their faculty/staff to mentor adult learners, commonly rely upon peer support, often through student cohort groups (sometimes referred to as a learning community). In a cohort group, fellow students collectively assist each individual within their group. Adult-focused institutions consciously augment these arrangements in ways to benefit individual adult learners.

Academic Support Services

An Adult Learning Focused Institution does not decline to help a potential student because he or she is not ready for college. Rather, the institution either provides resources to hone general academic skills or directs the student to those that can provide assistance in this area. The extent to which the institution is Adult Learning Focused is apparent through an evaluation of the impact of such support. Students who need academic help and commit to these programs before starting college classes are often strong performers in the classroom.

A telling sign of institutional commitment to the Student Support Systems Principle is the degree to which faculty members engage in coaching students on matters academic and otherwise. Faculty at an Adult Learning Focused Institution are aware of the resources available to support students and make an effort to connect students to them. Faculty at an ALFI make themselves available to students utilizing a variety of high-tech and low-tech options and resources to achieve good results, from e-mail and listservs to the telephone and face-to-face counseling in faculty offices or in the community.

Performance Indicators of This Principle in Action

An Adult Learning Focused Institution:

❖ Offers support (formal and informal) that is activated by a potential student's initial inquiry;

❖ Helps adults to become college-ready through existing academic support systems or in collaboration with other organizations;

❖ Devises flexible time frames for enrollment, registration, and program participation;

❖ Has faculty and staff who inform adult students about the institution's programs and services;

❖ Provides support services that address the life circumstances of the adult (e.g., child care, support networks, financing, adult-centered orientation and advising);

❖ Provides, or supports financially, professional development activities related to adult learning theory and application for faculty and staff;

❖ Requires that faculty/staff work with the community, employers, and/or unions to develop mentoring and advising programs;

❖ Works collaboratively with stakeholders to encourage employees/members to pursue their education and learning needs;
❖ Provides support for adult learners at times and places that are congruent with work schedules; and
❖ Works with stakeholders to establish education extension centers at or near work locations.

Best Practices or Examples of Evidence That May Demonstrate This Principle in Action

(see also Appendix B, Page References to the CAEL Benchmarking Study)

❖ Prospective student welcome center;
❖ Formal mentoring system using community-based professionals;
❖ Student cohort groups for program advancement/completion;
❖ Adult-centered services for students with adult responsibilities (childcare, etc);
❖ Off hours (non-daytime) student services options;
❖ "One-stop" centers where all administrative tasks can be completed;
❖ Call centers for student support systems;
❖ Adult Learner "liaison" to help with issues and problems at campus offices;
❖ Books delivered to the classroom or work/home of the adult learner;
❖ Learning assessment centers and/or web sites designed to assist adult learners and the institution to assess the learner's readiness for academic study;
❖ Remediation or college-preparatory courses;
❖ Allocation of a portion of faculty workload to advising and assessing adult learners;
❖ Resources dedicated to professional development activities for faculty and staff related to adult learning theory and its application; and
❖ Job descriptions for faculty and staff that clearly describe the importance of skills, knowledge, and experience in working with adult learners.

Student Support Systems

Example of the Principle in Action

Empire State College, State University of New York—Saratoga Springs, New York

DECENTRALIZED STUDENT SUPPORT SERVICES

Empire State College (ESC) establishes relationships with adult learners as early as possible to help them understand the demands and responsibilities of higher education and to determine how their goals and aspirations might be met by the programs and services offered at ESC. Early awareness on the part of institutions regarding students who need additional support and resources, especially with their writing skills, improves success rates and ensures a smoother path toward a degree.

The Virtual Student Center allows adult learners to conveniently perform various student services functions for themselves such as checking on financial aid status, registering on-line, obtaining program information, and communicating with faculty and staff. Empire State has also established the Writer's Complex, an on-line service to help students with their writing skills. It includes on-line text and interactive elements which enable adult learners to work through examples and receive immediate feedback.

Faculty perform a variety of roles such as advising prospective students, teaching, record keeping, participating in staff meetings, serving on committees, meeting with individual learners and evaluating prior learning portfolios. ESC is concerned with ensuring that new faculty members have the same dedication to adult learners as existing faculty. The college recruits nationally and seeks faculty who are looking to work in non-traditional adult education programs and who are dedicated to learner-centered rather than teacher centered-approaches. ESC is developing a systematic mentor development program for new faculty. Currently they employ a "buddy" system which pairs experienced faculty with new recruits.

From the CAEL Benchmarking Study, p. 86 (Flint & Associates, 1999).

Student Support Systems

Example of the Principle in Action

First Nations Technical Institute—Tyendinaga Mohawk Territory, Canada

THE TRAVELING COLLEGE

First Nations Technical Institute (FNTI) is an aboriginally owned and operated postsecondary institution located on the Tyendinaga Mohawk Territory in the Province of Ontario, Canada. Founded in 1985, FNTI offers degrees, diplomas and certificates in human services, small business management, computer science, media studies, aviation, public administration, literacy, and secondary school graduation. The majority of the Institute's postsecondary diploma programs are offered to employed adult learners who live and work in rural and urban centers scattered mainly through Ontario, and to a lesser extent across Canada. Many learners reside in remote, isolated northern locations.

As a response to the diverse learning needs of adults living in First Nations communities, a group of skilled, committed Aboriginal faculty working for FNTI, and living in their own communities across Ontario, designed culturally-based programs and courses in a variety of human service areas. In order to deliver these programs, faculty and support staff regularly face extensive travel because courses are delivered as close as possible to where learners live and work.

Course delivery is offered in a variety of non-traditional formats. The most commonly used method involves delivering a two-year, full-time diploma program over a period of three years, enabling learners to continue working while earning the credential. This model is based on three or four intensive, week long courses per year over the three-year period.

The program team meets with learners at a central location for the weeklong sessions. Learners influence the selection of location, timing and content of each of the sessions. Learning resources—including reference texts, videos, etc.—are also taken to these sessions. Occasionally, learners take their children along with them to sessions. Child care arrangements are made at the facility in which the courses are being held. Often sessions will take place at a hotel but, when feasible, local community facilities are utilized.

In addition to the individual support offered by the program delivery team, learners are also helped to form regional tutorial groups. Use of telephones, fax machines, and e-mail helps students to maintain regular contact. The use of web-based course delivery and tutorials has been limited due to lack of availability in remote locations. An elder of the community is an important part of the delivery team, working closely with the program faculty and staff, traveling with them to all of the course sessions, and providing important cultural teaching and counseling.

Contributed by Paul Zakos, Manager of Program Development and Prior Learning Assessment at First Nations Technical Institute.

A Story about Student Support Services

Some colleges have outcomes that just defy prediction. By all accounts, Robert Morris College (RMC) in Illinois should not be achieving the results that it does, given its environment and circumstances. The main campus of RMC is located in Chicago, a city whose public schools face enormous challenges to improve educational achievement and accountability. In the early 1990s, the U.S. Secretary of Education called the Chicago public school system "the worst in America." While great progress has been made since then, the average ACT score of the city's 50 public high schools is 17.5, which is considerably lower than the national average. RMC attracts a student body in which 49 percent of the enrollment at the Chicago campus are graduates of the Chicago public school system. Institutionally, approximately 39 percent of the students are African-American and about 26 percent are Hispanic. In addition, the majority of students are first generation college students and more than half are self-supporting adults, working full time while completing their college studies.

Yet, in 2000, an analysis by the independent journal *Black Issues in Higher Education* found that Robert Morris College graduates more minorities with associate degrees than any other college in the nation, regardless of institution size. This is accomplished despite the fact that as a private, non-profit institution, RMC tuition is four times higher than nearby city colleges, the names of which do not appear on the journal's list of the top fifty producers of associate degrees for African-Americans. RMC can also show that it graduates more minorities with bachelor's degrees in Business than any other institution in the state of Illinois. Recently, the College was also recognized in a study supported by the Chicagoland Chamber of Commerce as a leader in technology.

In 1999–2000, the associate degree graduation rate at RMC was 78 percent. That year, the institutional job placement rate into entry-level positions was 97 percent. In 1992, the regional accrediting commission for RMC approved the college's first baccalaureate offering, and has subsequently approved additional applied baccalaureate programs in Graphic Arts and Computer Studies. While these new offerings required a substantial investment in quality faculty and support, it did not prevent RMC from expanding the Chicago campus capacity by moving to a new facility in 1998. Moreover, it added new suburban campuses in Orland Park and Naperville in 1992 and 1998, respectively.

While academic quality is put first and foremost at RMC, a series of effective and efficient student support services is what delivers these remarkable outcomes. Telling the whole story of that system is beyond the scope of what can be done in this workbook. Know this much, though: Just as important as having a *system* for student support is a *climate* that treats each student with the utmost respect and concern. At RMC the climate that has permeated the institution is that of having a welcoming attitude and a supportive, caring environment.

Flint, Tom. Interview with Deborah Dahlen-Zelechowski, Senior Vice President for Advancement, Robert Morris College.

STUDENT SUPPORT SYSTEMS PRINCIPLE ACTIVITY

To evaluate the extent to which your institution is implementing practices that relate to this Principle, you may wish to complete the informal *Institutional Self-Assessment Worksheet* which follows this explanation.

As you work your way through the worksheet pay particular attention to the Best Practices Performance Indicators and use them to help you reflect upon the practices at your own institution. The Performance Indicators on the worksheet are by no means inclusive of all possible indicators. Feel free to add performance indicators not listed on the sheet but used at your institution.

Using the Worksheet

As you look at individual or groups of performance indicators, make decisions about whether or not there is evidence of the Principle in practice at your college or university. The worksheet has a three-step process. First, mark the appropriate column: *Yes (Y), NO (N),* and *Under Development (UD).* Next, write down what person or unit is responsible for making sure that the appropriate practice, process or procedure happens. Finally, cite the evidence to support your evaluation.

1. **To decide which column to mark (Y, N, or UD), consider these criteria: Is the evidence supporting your decision:**

   a. **Valid?** Does it relate directly to this Principle and the Performance Indicators?

   b. **Sufficient?** Does it show broad and consistent presence in your institution (depending upon how broadly you have defined the "institution" here)?

   c. **Current?** Is it observable today? Will it be observable tomorrow?

   d. **Authentic?** Is it genuine? Is it accurate? Is it sufficiently plentiful to be considered representative of typical institutional practice?

   Tip: Use the "Under Development" column for items whose status is currently unknown, or whose plans are in progress but not yet implemented. Consider these high priority items, the status of which should be revisited by the team quickly.

2. Regardless of how the evidence meets the above criteria, ask: **Who performs—or should perform—the activities or procedures entailed by the Performance Indicators?** Identify the unit(s) or person(s). If those units/persons are not participating in this activity, then they may need to be recruited for purposes of obtaining information needed here, or for implementing an improvement strategy.

3. Cite the evidence that relates to your evaluation in the Y/N/UD columns. Avoid using evidence rooted only in personal, subjective judgement. **What concrete, tangible evidence may others observe to substantiate your decision?**

STUDENT SUPPORT SYSTEMS PRINCIPLE

The institution assists adult learners using comprehensive academic and student support systems in order to enhance students' capacities to become self-directed lifelong learners.

Legend:

Y = Yes
N = No
UD = Under Development

PERFORMANCE INDICATORS	Y	N	UD	UNIT/PERSON RESPONSIBLE	EVIDENCE
Exemplary practice supporting this Principle occurs when an institution:					
• Offers a support system activated by a potential student's initial inquiry about the institution.					
• Helps adults become college-ready by offering academic support or in collaboration with other organizations.					
• Devises flexible time frames for enrollment, registration and program participation.					
• Has faculty and staff who help adult learners connect with academic and support services.					
• Provides support services that address the life circumstances of the adult (e.g. child care, support networks, financing, adult-centered orientation, and advising).					
• Provides, or supports financially, professional development activities related to adult learning theory and application for faculty and staff.					
• Requires that faculty/staff work with the community, employers and/or unions to develop mentoring and advising programs.					
• Works collaboratively with stakeholders to encourage their employees/members to pursue their education and learning needs.					
• Provides support for adult learners at times and places that are congruent with work schedules.					
• Works with stakeholders to establish education extension centers at or near work locations.					

See Glossary in Appendix F for Definitions

Chapter 10

The Technology Principle

Principle

The institution uses information technology to provide relevant and timely information to enhance the learning experience.

Digital information technology (IT) is the chalkboard of tomorrow. Increasingly, as homes, workplaces, and marketplaces become wired and the information therein digitized; as the power and connectivity of desktop, laptop, and palmtop devices grows; and as the communities of connected peoples enlarge worldwide, then we will witness quantum leaps in learning communities.

To the extent that higher education hinges upon the effective communication of information among people, improvements in IT tools and similar innovations augurs well for expanding access and success to all—including adult learners. Considering the rapid development and spread of IT tools, it is likely that the continued availability of online texts, documents, images, sounds, videos, simulations, and Internet search engines will revolutionize our assumptions about the process of education.

Colleges and universities can use information technology to improve administrative and student support functions, and to enhance the delivery of courses and learning opportunities. The technology can be simple or sophisticated. Regardless of its purpose or level of complexity, Adult Learning Focused Institutions (ALFIs) see information technology as a means to helping adults to manage their learning so they can succeed and achieve their goals.

Information Technology Can Provide Greater Access and Save Time

When IT enhanced learning and information permeates the institution, it creates a more user-friendly environment for the adult learner. In this respect, one of the most important functions of information technologies is in their time-saving dimension. Online learning and student support programs expand access for students who might be isolated geographically, or who may otherwise be place-bound, by circumventing the travel times that used to be mandatory. Such time-based requirements run the gamut from students in rural locations who cannot take the time to travel to the nearest campus, to students who prefer to access material in the college or university library in the middle of the night. Technology enhanced services also mean that student services ranging from admissions to writing tutors can be accessed by adult students at times and places convenient for them, from anywhere that they can access the Internet, thus allowing them to better manage the progress of their learning.

Information Technology Expands the Breadth and Depth of Subjects Studied

A further time-saving benefit springing from IT is the ability to enhance learning by focusing on concepts and how to use them, rather than on techniques. For example, prior to the advent of personal computers and the software packages written to run on them, the performance of certain sophisticated statistical routines, such as multiple regression, were extremely laborious. Now that such statistical procedures are readily available on small computers, the focus of instruction can shift away from having to monitor the accurate performance of repetitive calculations to the conceptual underpinnings of the procedure itself. The faculty can now focus on what the procedure means, when to use it, and why it is valuable.

Technologically assisted tutoring programs are another example of how IT can enhance the learning experience. These programs provide an endless number of problems for students to work on, offering step-by-step explanations of student errors as they occur. These types of programs provide a comfortable learning environment in subjects like mathematics, which are problematic for many adult learners. The tutorials allow students to work at their own pace and at times convenient for them, as well as allowing the instructor to center his or her attention on course content and usability.

Information Technology Opens Opportunities for Learning Groups for Adults

Adult learners often conduct their academic studies in relative isolation from the rest of the learners in the academic institution in which they are enrolled. This is the case because they are typically only on campus to attend classes or to receive academic and support services. In addition, many adult programs feature shortened class timeframes, making it difficult for adult learners to have contact with one another between class meetings. The pressure of balancing academic responsibilities with work and family further exacerbates time constraints. Although collaboration with fellow students is particularly important to adult learners, it is often difficult to arrange due to these constraints.

Information technology holds the promise of bringing adult learners closer to their academic communities. Whether it is simple e-mail correspondence or an online course, for many adult learners technology can make the difference between working alone and learning from others. The use of e-mail, course web sites, online discussion boards, online chats, and course management systems extends the classroom beyond the physical borders of the campus. The appropriate use of these and similar electronic teaching and learning tools means that learners' interactions with one another, with the instructor, and with other learning resources—things that were once restricted to the on-campus learner—are available without restriction to time and place.

Performance Indicators of This Principle in Action

An Adult Learning Friendly Institution:

❖ Develops and implements technology competence standards for all learners, including adults;

❖ Uses technology to build and reinforce a sense of community among adult learners;

❖ Provides sufficient support for faculty and staff to develop skills in the use of technologies that will facilitate e-learning and electronically delivered student services;

❖ Ensures that all vital administrative functions—from admissions to alumni services—are available online, allowing access from any Internet connected computer;

❖ Uses information technology to enable adult learners to assess their own learning needs and their learning process;

❖ Ensures that adults have opportunities to discover whether an electronically delivered program is appropriate for them;

❖ Supports the integration of e-learning modules, techniques, and tools into all programming; and

❖ Employs technology to complement the technology-rich environment in which many adults work.

Best Practices or Examples of Evidence That May Demonstrate This Principle in Action
(see also Appendix B, Page References to the CAEL Benchmarking Study)

❖ Existence of web/e-mail computer orientation sessions for adult learners in relation to the institution's systems, including distribution of access codes, software, and arranging e-mail accounts;

❖ An up-to-date web site containing information about programs and opportunities for communication by learners with faculty, staff and fellow learners;

❖ A schedule of web-board meeting sessions for adult learners to encourage ongoing communication and to provide flexibility and support;

❖ A list of e-mail addresses provided for all adult learners that includes peers, faculty, staff, community, and business contacts;

❖ Lists of various web-site locations which offer self-assessment rubrics, learning style inventories, and educational resources for adult learners;

❖ Processes which offer adult learners the option of registering and taking part in counseling sessions in person, on-line, or at designated off-campus locations at times convenient for them;

❖ Programs/courses that provide adult learners with the option of taking classes on-line, on-campus, or a combination of the two;

❖ Classrooms that have up-to-date technology used primarily to help adult learners achieve their education and career goals;

❖ Online library resources that can be accessed from any Internet connected computer;

❖ Existence of a long-range information technology plan to ensure that appropriate technology is purchased to expand the learning opportunities for adult learners;

❖ Technology orientation sessions available to all entering adult students so that they may use the institution's information technology confidently;

❖ Faculty training programs or professional development funds for faculty for technology-supported instruction;

❖ Electronic information services (Financial aid, admission, etc);

❖ Institution-originated telephonic student contacts; and

❖ Student, faculty, and administrator networking via e-mail.

References

Flint, Thomas A. & Associates. (1999). *Best Practices in Adult Learning: A CAEL/APQC Benchmarking Study*. Chicago: Council for Adult and Experiential Learning.

Schank, Roger C. (1997). *Virtual Learning: A Revolutionary Approach to Building a Highly Skilled Workforce*. New York: McGraw-Hill.

The Technology Principle

Example of the Principle in Action

University of Maryland University College—Adelphi, Maryland

The University of Maryland University College (UMUC) is one of the eleven degree-granting institutions in the University of Maryland System. Yet it is most remarkable among the host of state-supported universities in that it is primarily devoted to serving adult, part-time students through high quality educational programs. Since its founding more than 50 years ago, it has been a preeminent provider of degrees through distance learning. In its latest form, distance learning takes place via online degree programs. This means that UMUC has surpassed nearly all other universities worldwide in its online program offerings: more than two dozen bachelor's and master's degree programs that can be completed entirely at a distance.

UMUC provides an undergraduate education to students from dozens of countries. It also offers postsecondary programs to members of the U.S. armed services and their families through more than 160 locations around the world. Since the online programs of UMUC support tens of thousands of course enrollments annually—in rapidly escalating number—the University uses a variety of technologies to communicate with its students. The heart of its educational technology is WebTycho, its interactive classroom software. Needless to say, technological supports permeate every aspect of UMUC, including processes of admission, registration, and advising, to name a few.

The popularity of UMUC programs with adults is due in no small degree to the expressed value of flexibility on the part of the institution when serving adults. In part, the UMUC 'Statement of Values' reads,

> "We exist to serve our students in times and places convenient to them, and to enable them to achieve their learning objectives with minimal non-academic obstacles... We take the degree to the student, geographically or situationally. We use every feasible instructional delivery mechanism or platform to extend our degree opportunities to our students."

Flexibility and convenience are key indicators for access to adult learners, especially if they are employed. UMUC explicitly celebrates that connection:

> "We define value as 'relevance' to our students. And, for most of those customers, relevance translates to 'development of the workforce... We stand for providing gateways of opportunity for those students who missed their chance for a college education during the traditional college-age years."

Adapted from information available at www.umuc.edu.

The Technology Principle

Example of the Principle in Action

Rio Salado Community College—Tempe, Arizona

At first glance, many of the features of most community colleges—physical facilities, curricula, and the like—make them appear similar to more traditional institutions of higher education. In the case of Rio Salado, the College bills itself as "the college without walls." Technology is a key part of Rio Salado College's strategy to be a leading choice for adult learners.

Rio Salado was founded in 1978 with the explicit purpose of serving working adults and, therefore, has pioneered flexible educational opportunities for adults using a variety of communication technologies. Prospective students may learn about Rio Salado by exploring its virtual Visitors' Center located on the Rio Salado web site. From the web site, a visitor may download an electronic file in RealMedia file format that tells the story of Rio Salado as a video presentation.

Although it has administrative offices, Rio Salado does not maintain a traditional campus. The College's face-to-face classes can be conducted from a variety of sites that include corporations, government agencies, and community centers with which the college collaborates. Some sites include the Paradise Valley Shopping Mall and Luke Air Force Base.

In 1996, Rio Salado became the first Arizona college to offer Internet-based courses. All student services to support those courses are also online, including the functions of registration, tutoring, advising, and library services. Today, the College offers as many as 200 courses online, and through its efforts has garnered numerous awards for its distance learning operations, including:

- Outstanding Web Site in Higher Education, from the North American Web Association;
- Paragon Award for Most Creative Use of Technology, from the National Council of Marketing and Public Relations; and
- Award of Excellence for Distance Learning, from the Council for Advancement and Support of Education.

By offering courses in accelerated formats, Rio Salado assures flexibility and convenience for adult learners. Rio Salado goes further to ensure that lifelong learning opportunities continue for its graduates, by having arranged for full recognition of its credits and programs with other institutions offering distance learning degree programs, including Capella University, Charter Oak State College, Governors State University, Jones International University, Marylhurst University, SUNY Empire State College, University of Phoenix, and Western Governors University.

Adapted from information available at http://www.rio.maricopa.edu/.

TECHNOLOGY PRINCIPLE ACTIVITY

To evaluate the extent to which your institution is implementing practices that relate to this Principle, you may wish to complete the informal *Institutional Self-Assessment Worksheet* which follows this explanation.

As you work your way through the worksheet pay particular attention to the Best Practices Performance Indicators and use them to help you reflect upon the practices at your own institution. The Performance Indicators on the worksheet are by no means inclusive of all possible indicators. Feel free to add performance indicators not listed on the sheet but used at your institution.

Using the Worksheet

As you look at individual or groups of performance indicators, make decisions about whether or not there is evidence of the Principle in practice at your college or university. The worksheet has a three-step process. First, mark the appropriate column: *Yes (Y)*, *No (N)* and *Under Development (UD)*. Next, write down what person or unit is responsible for making sure that the appropriate practice, process or procedure happens. Finally, cite the evidence to support your evaluation.

1. **To decide which column to mark (Y, N, or UD), consider these criteria: Is the evidence supporting your decision:**

    a. **Valid?** Does it relate directly to this Principle and the Performance Indicators?

    b. **Sufficient?** Does it show broad and consistent presence in your institution (depending upon how broadly you have defined the "institution" here)?

    c. **Current?** Is it observable today? Will it be observable tomorrow?

    d. **Authentic?** Is it genuine? Is it accurate? Is it sufficiently plentiful to be considered representative of typical institutional practice?

    Tip: Use the "Under Development" column for items whose status is currently unknown, or whose plans are in progress but not yet implemented. Consider these high priority items, the status of which should be revisited by the team quickly.

2. Regardless of how the evidence meets the above criteria, ask: **Who performs—or should perform—the activities or procedures entailed by the Performance Indicators?** Identify the unit(s) or person(s). If those units/persons are not participating in this activity, then they may need to be recruited for purposes of obtaining information needed here, or for implementing an improvement strategy.

3. Cite the evidence that relates to your evaluation in the Y/N/UD columns. Avoid using evidence rooted only in personal, subjective judgement. **What concrete, tangible evidence may others observe to substantiate your decision?**

TECHNOLOGY PRINCIPLE

The institution uses information technology to provide relevant and timely information and to enhance the learning experience.

Legend:

Y = Yes
N = No
UD = Under Development

PERFORMANCE INDICATORS	Y	N	UD	UNIT/PERSON RESPONSIBLE	EVIDENCE
Exemplary practice supporting this Principle occurs when an institution:					
• Provides technology orientation to all entering adult learners so that technology can be used confidently and competently.					
• Uses technology to build and reinforce community among adult learners.					
• Uses information technology to provide flexible and timely education and administrative services (e.g. web registration systems, call centers).					
• Uses information technology to enable adult learners to assess their own learning needs and their learning process.					
• Uses technology to expand the choices of learning styles/options (e.g. partial and full Internet-based courses, technology-rich on-campus instruction).					
• Employs technology to complement the technology-rich environment in which many adults work.					

See Glossary in Appendix F for Definitions

Chapter 11

The Strategic Partnerships Principle

Principle

The institution engages in strategic relationships, partnerships, and collaborations with employers and other organizations in order to develop and improve educational opportunities for adult learners.

Educational benefits can be a valuable incentive in attracting workers. They can also signify an employer's desire to remain competitive and to ensure that the abilities of employees continue to grow. As we experience a shift from an industry-based to a knowledge-based economy, institutions of higher education are being seen as a critical component to economic success. Educating the traditional aged student for a future workforce is always important. But what is equally important is that by the year 2005, 48 percent of the U.S. labor force will be between the ages of 35 and 55 (Oblinger & Verville, p. 6). Therefore, it is to the advantage of business and industry to invest in the education of incumbent workers.

Employers, industry groups, and labor unions can be seen as natural allies of colleges and universities. Each needs the valuable skills and abilities that a college education provides to members of the workforce. And, each is interested in supporting colleges and universities in what they do best—educating people who can adeptly apply their knowledge and skill on the job. For example, as fewer and fewer jobs or career paths come with a lifetime guarantee, far-sighted labor leaders now promote bargained-for education benefits as a prime ingredient for the success of workers. Another example is the growing number of private-sector led, skills consortia that are being organized around regional industry clusters to address the specific skill needs of those clusters, particularly in advanced technology, health care, and education.

The workplace is an obvious venue for introducing higher education opportunities to adult learners, just as the high school is the natural site for introducing higher education to 18-year olds. In fact, working adults could be the largest untapped market of potential college students. Although ambitious working adults will often find their own way to an institution of higher learning, many more do not think of themselves as "college material." Yet, with a concerted effort on the part of employers, labor unions, community-based organizations and colleges, these reluctant adults can successfully earn a degree. Colleges and universities can remove many of the barriers that keep working adults from formal education by making programs convenient and relevant through on-site recruitment, advising, admissions, support services and creating learning activities that relate key course concepts to workplace and community issues. Employers and other stake-holders can create an environment that keeps adult learners motivated and invested in their education by encouraging supervisor support, offering opportunities to practice newly gained knowledge, making resources available for educational activities, and communicating the relationship between education and career opportunities. When combined, these add up to a powerful and effective model for adult learner success.

Awarding credit towards degrees for college-level learning obtained in the workplace is also critical to effective strategic partnerships. Not only can institutions offer programs of prior learning assessment (PLA) (based on portfolios or on institutional evaluations of corporate educational programs), they can also collaborate with employers to positively promote such programs within the workplace as a means of encouraging employed adults to return to formal learning.

The Adult Learning Focused Institution (ALFI) welcomes the involvement of employers, unions and community-based organizations in making academic programs available to workers. In fact, an ALFI views these relationships as an effective way to carry its mission to the community. By working in tandem with stakeholders to make appropriate educational resources available to learners, the ALFI fosters an environment in which everybody wins: the learner, the stakeholder, and the institution.

Performance Indicators of This Principle in Action

An Adult Learning Focused Institution:

* Promotes use of prior learning assessment to employers and community organizations;
* Recruits learners through various stakeholder groups (e.g., businesses, unions, and community-based organizations);
* Collaborates with stakeholders to help establish learning goals that fulfill skill needs and lead to career opportunities;
* Works with stakeholders to develop mentoring and advising programs;
* Promotes recognition of learning that comes from training and education programs outside the college or university (ACE, CLEP, DANTES);
* Collaborates with stakeholders to develop ways to encourage their employees or members to pursue an education;
* Encourages employers to make a variety of company resources available to employees for education related activities; and
* Works with stakeholders to measure the impact of education programs on their goals.

Best Practices or Examples of Evidence That May Demonstrate This Principle in Action
(see also Appendix B, Page References to the CAEL Benchmarking Study)

* Discounted tuition rates for companies, unions, or community-based organizations with multiple employees/members enrolled in the institution's degree/certificate programs;
* Collaborative projects with stakeholders that support and promote lifelong learning for all of their employees and/or members;
* Curricular learning goals that meet stakeholder learning/training goals;
* On-site (i.e., at the workplace and in the community) delivery of courses and support services, including recruiting, advising, and instruction;
* Professionals from business and labor acting as mentors and advisors for adult learners;

❖ Programs that require faculty to engage in professional/business learning environments related to their discipline;

❖ Dedicated institutional staff doing employer outreach;

❖ Adjunct faculty appointments from partnering employers & employment sectors;

❖ Studies of the Return on Investment in Learning (ROI-L) for partnering organizations;

❖ Assessment of worker employability traits at partnering organizations;

❖ Employability or workplace readiness guarantee for graduates; and

❖ Utilization of partner resources (e.g., employer's space, equipment, or trainers/instructors).

References

Flint, Thomas A. (1999). *Best Practices in Adult Learning: A CAEL/APQC Benchmarking Study.* Chicago: Council for Adult and Experiential Learning.

Oblinger, Diana G. and Verville, Anne-Lee. (1998). *What Business Wants from Higher Education.* Phoenix, AZ: The Oryx Press/American Council on Education Series on Higher Education.

Strategic Partnerships Principle

Examples of the Principle in Action

Central Michigan University—Mt. Pleasant, Michigan

BACHELOR OF SCIENCE IN VEHICLE DESIGN DEGREE PROGRAM

Foretelling a trend for the future, many jobs currently require increasingly sophisticated skill sets. A perfect example can be found with those who design automobiles. For decades, vehicle design was largely a matter of drafting skills: technicians who followed the direction of engineers to create two-dimensional drawings using paper, pencil, and drafting tools. Much needed knowledge was acquired on the job from peers, from highly-educated engineers, and, sometimes, from non-credit instruction. Yet, today as the technologies within automobiles rapidly evolve, so too does the role of those who design them: the designer must now be a highly skilled computer technologist who can create three-dimensional designs and apply advanced engineering principles.

When Detroit automakers sought new approaches from higher education to fulfill their workplace needs for vehicle designers, Central Michigan University alone was willing to create a new degree program from the ground up. All existing structures and assumptions were set aside. CMU obtained participation of faculty and administrators from its College of Extended Learning and from the Industrial and Engineering Technology department, and it accomplished what few might have expected. Over a period of six months involving active collaboration with the automobile manufacturers, the program was rolled out. Features of the program include:

- 124 credit hours for the degree;
- Accelerated course formats over five eight-week semesters;
- Distance learning components for flexible self-paced instruction;
- Prior learning assessment provisions;
- World-class expertise from the industry to deliver instruction and mentor students; and
- Frequent and rigorous assessment of student and employer satisfaction with the delivery of the program.

CMU is candid in disclosing that such collaboration is not without challenges. Among the challenges:

- Culture shock—academic and corporate settings move at different paces and speak different languages;
- Budget stress—costs of building innovative projects are difficult to predict; and
- Leadership—success comes from having champions to lead the cause.

Yet, CMU is certain to claim that this program is one of its most recent and worthy accomplishments in the matter of strategic partnerships.

Clark, Deborah; Jelnicki, James; Sprague, David; & Ivanitskaya, Lana. (2001). When academics and executives collide: How CMU teamed with auto industry experts to create an award-winning degree in vehicle design. *CAEL Forum and News*, 24 (3), 16-18.

Strategic Partnerships Principle

Examples of the Principle in Action

Baldwin-Wallace College—Berea, Ohio

THE GATEWAY CERTIFICATE

As many areas of the United States prepare to cope with what has been referred to as the 'echo boom'—that is, the children of the baby boomers who were born after World War II—critical shortages of teachers have developed or are anticipated in many school districts. The planned retirement of many current teachers only aggravates the problem. To address the problem locally, two divisions within Baldwin-Wallace College—Lifelong Learning and Education—began a collaboration to prepare more teachers and instructional support staff by using incumbent workers in non-teaching roles from within the local districts. Called the "Gateway Certificate" program, the College began its first partnership in May, 2000 with the Berea, Ohio school district to prepare "classified staff" (such as school bus drivers, custodians, cafeteria workers, and office staff) for future instructional roles. The fact that many of these classified workers have substantial educational work to complete before being qualified as teachers has not dampened their enthusiasm; in Berea, some 176 employees out of a corps of 800 initially expressed a desire to enroll in the program. In fact, the ability to earn a pre-baccalaureate certificate in about one year's time gives students tangible evidence of their abilities as lifelong learners.

The program combines on-site instruction in the school districts with accelerated formats, alternating two- and three-credit hours courses over the period of a year, culminating in a certificate representing five courses that satisfy some core requirements needed by learners who wish to pursue a formal teaching degree. The program deepens the existing commitment of employees within these school districts, whose loyalty is strengthened even as they personally explore their potential for a postsecondary degree in a context that is responsive to their needs.

Besides the advantages to adult learners and the school districts in which they work, the College benefits by strengthening its community roots and forging working partnerships that will provide a pipeline of potential degree-seeking students for both its Lifelong Learning and Education divisions.

Bash, Lee & Higgerson, Mary Lou. (2002). The Gateway Certificate: School staff become adult degree students. *CAEL Forum & News*, 25 (2), 18-19.

A Story about Strategic Partnerships

The tenth largest airline in the world carries no passengers. That did not stop it from building a 2.7 million square foot facility at the airport in Louisville, Kentucky.

This company moves parcels, not people. UPS delivers more than 12.5 million air express and ground packages each day. In 1998, the company announced that Louisville would be the site of its new cutting-edge, automated sorting facility. The new center nearly doubled UPS's capability in Louisville and requires 6,000 new employees to make it run.

UPS currently employs more than 15,000 in Louisville, already making it one of the largest employers in Jefferson County. However, when the announcement to expand was made, Louisville was experiencing a labor shortage and city and county officials were concerned that UPS might look elsewhere for its expansion efforts.

To attract potential employees to UPS, the University of Louisville, Jefferson County Community College, and Jefferson Technical College joined with the Governor's office to form the Metropolitan College, a unique collaborative with UPS. Metropolitan College offers classes that fit worker's schedules along with special services and educational benefits. It is a win-win situation because UPS gets its workforce needs met and Kentucky residents get the benefit of an education. Since the program began, more than 2,000 students have enrolled.

Metropolitan College has brought changes to all of the participating institutions. For example, the University of Louisville developed a student residence dedicated to serving UPS workers. Special shuttle busses now operate between the campus and the airport, and some classes are conducted during the middle of the night to accommodate work shifts.

Recently, this model program has expanded to meet the community's need for healthcare workers. Scholarships to Metropolitan College are now being offered by Norton Healthcare to help students train as nurses and health care technicians. Health care students will work for UPS and attend classes the first year. After that, students will go to school full time and have the opportunity to work at UPS or Norton.

Notes:
- "Health-care Worker Shortage Prompts Norton to Offer $600,000 in scholarships" *The Louisville Courier-Journal*, June 9, 2000.
- "UPS Builds a College in Kentucky" UPS Press Release www.community.ups.com/community/resources/helping/kentucky.html.

STRATEGIC PARTNERSHIPS PRINCIPLE ACTIVITY

To evaluate the extent to which your institution is implementing practices that relate to this Principle, you may wish to complete the informal *Institutional Self-Assessment Worksheet* which follows this explanation.

As you work your way through the worksheet pay particular attention to the Best Practices Performance Indicators and use them to help you reflect upon the practices at your own institution. The Performance Indicators on the worksheet are by no means inclusive of all possible indicators. Feel free to add performance indicators not listed on the sheet but used at your institution.

Using the Worksheet

As you look at individual or groups of performance indicators, make decisions about whether or not there is evidence of the Principle in practice at your college or university. The worksheet has a three-step process. First, mark the appropriate column: *Yes (Y), No (N)* and *Under Development (UD)*. Next, write down what person or unit is responsible for making sure that the appropriate practice, process or procedure happens. Finally, cite the evidence to support your evaluation.

1. **To decide which column to mark (Y, N, or UD), consider these criteria: Is the evidence supporting your decision:**

   a. **Valid?** Does it relate directly to this Principle and the Performance Indicators?

   b. **Sufficient?** Does it show broad and consistent presence in your institution (depending upon how broadly you have defined the "institution" here)?

   c. **Current?** Is it observable today? Will it be observable tomorrow?

   d. **Authentic?** Is it genuine? Is it accurate? Is it sufficiently plentiful to be considered representative of typical institutional practice?

   Tip: Use the "Under Development" column for items whose status is currently unknown, or whose plans are in progress but not yet implemented. Consider these high priority items, the status of which should be revisited by the team quickly.

2. Regardless of how the evidence meets the above criteria, ask: **Who performs—or should perform—the activities or procedures entailed by the Performance Indicators?** Identify the unit(s) or person(s). If those units/persons are not participating in this activity, then they may need to be recruited for purposes of obtaining information needed here, or for implementing an improvement strategy.

3. Cite the evidence that relates to your evaluation in the Y/N/UD columns. Avoid using evidence rooted only in personal, subjective judgement. **What concrete, tangible evidence may others observe to substantiate your decision?**

STRATEGIC PARTNERSHIPS PRINCIPLE

The institution engages in strategic relationships, partnerships, and collaborations with employers and other organizations to develop and improve educational opportunities for adult learners.

Legend:

Y = Yes
N = No
UD = Under Development

PERFORMANCE INDICATORS	Y	N	UD	UNIT/PERSON RESPONSIBLE	EVIDENCE
Exemplary practice supporting this Principle occurs when an institution:					
• Promotes use of prior learning assessment to employers and community organizations.					
• Recruits learners through various stakeholder groups (e.g., businesses, unions, and community-based organizations).					
• Collaborates with stakeholders to help establish learning goals that fulfill skill needs and lead to career opportunities.					
• Works with stakeholders to develop mentoring and advising programs.					
• Promotes recognition of learning that comes from training and education programs outside the college or university (ACE, CLEP, DANTES).					
• Collaborates with stakeholders to develop ways to encourage their employees or members to pursue an education.					
• Encourages employers to make a variety of company resources available to employees for education related activities.					
• Works with stakeholders to measure the impact of education programs on their goals.					

See Glossary in Appendix F for Definitions

Chapter 12

How Well Are You Doing?

Assessing Your Institution's Services to Adult Learners

Upon completion of the institutional self-assessment process, you will likely be eager to determine the extent to which your institution fares in relation to the eight Principles of Effectiveness identified by CAEL. In reviewing the assessment results for each of the Principles and their Performance Indicators you may wish to consider the following questions:

1. How many of the stated performance criteria for each of the eight key *Principles of Effectiveness* were you able to document as being present at your institution?

2. How many of the eight key *Principles of Effectiveness* did you assess as being under development at your institution?

3. Were you able to identify other performance indicators and/or *Principles of Effectiveness* not covered in the self-assessment scale that are indicative of exemplary practices at your institution?

4. Did you uncover any major gaps in services to adult learners at your institution as a result of the institutional self-assessment process?

5. Will you be able to use the results of the institutional self-assessment process to set some priorities for further action related to improving services to adult learners at your institution? Have you given any thought to what might be the next steps in that process?

Performing the institutional self-assessment process and reflecting upon the implications for your institution may have helped you become more aware that assisting adults in meeting their learning needs is best seen as a collaborative, ongoing process.

Did the institutional self-assessment process provide you with any new insights and/or pleasant surprises about the way in which your institution helps adults meet their learning needs? Did you discover any new adult learner advocates or champions? Were you able to generate greater interest in the plight of adult learners and increase the momentum for change?

You may have noticed, for example, that many of the performance indicators apply to several of the *Principles of Effectiveness* in significant ways. For example, some of the key performance indicators that are securely intertwined with most of the *Principles of Effectiveness* are: engaging adult learners collaboratively in life and career planning, identifying and assessing learning outcomes, designing and delivering flexible curricula, and developing strategic partnerships. For high performing Adult Learning Focused Institutions (ALFIs), the key performance indicators represent minimum standards of practice. Genuinely accepting adult learners as true partners in the educational enterprise and cooperatively planning with them enables Adult Learning Focused

Institutions to ensure that a process of continuous improvement will be present at their institutions. Adult learners offer rich and diverse experiences, skills, knowledge, and perceptions about the communities in which they live, the changing nature of work, and about the larger society.

Adult Learning Focused Institutions, by their very existence, challenge many of the fundamental assumptions about the nature of learning and teaching. The eight key *Principles of Effectiveness* and their Performance Indicators provide concrete proof that the focus of educational practice in these institutions has moved away from control and authority to a more democratic, participatory, and learning-centered approach. They not only acknowledge the legitimacy of the important learning needs of adult citizens, they also accept them as partners in the planning, delivery, and evaluation of their own learning.

We trust that the time and energy you devote to performing the institutional self-assessment is worthwhile and productive. The performance indicators that support the eight *Principles of Effectiveness* clearly highlight two important points about ALFIs. The first is that they respond to the educational needs of adults in a variety of distinctive and forward-thinking ways. The second is that their unique institutional responses are supported by a common set of beliefs, principles, and a shared vision which places the needs of adult learners at the core of the institution's mission, rather than on the margins. It is our firm belief that using this workbook can help you sharpen your institution's focus in serving adult learners in much the same fashion.

The Force Field Analysis

After completing the informal institutional self-assessment process, you and your team will hopefully have more clearly identified gaps in services and/or areas needing to be strengthened. In addition to the institutional self-assessment, another tool which you may find helpful in your evaluation is the Force Field Analysis, developed several years ago by psychologist Kurt Lewin.

The Force Field Analysis provides a practical framework for problem-solving and for implementing planned changes in organizations. Figure 12-1, on page ##, provides a preliminary assessment of the challenges involved in helping your institution become more adult learning focused. The top and bottom of Figure 12-1 represent opposite ends of the continuum in relation to how well your institution serves adult learners using the eight key *Principles of Effectiveness* as the benchmarks against which to measure its services and any changes that are made. The environmental conditions and pressures in your institution which support an ALFI approach are identified as the driving forces represented by the arrows pushing upward. The arrows pushing downward represent the restraining forces which are keeping your institution from moving toward a more complete and open response to helping adult learners meet their learning needs. The length of each of the arrows can be used by you and your team to indicate the relative strength of the positive forces driving change for adult learners or the forces preventing those changes from occurring. The *equilibrium*, which is represented by the horizontal line toward which all of the arrows are pointing, can be changed in the direction of greater responsiveness to the needs of adult learners. One way is to strengthen or add forces in the direction of change; another way is to reduce or remove some of the restraining forces by changing the direction of the forces. One of the most efficient ways to bring about change is to change the direction of one of the forces. Thus the removal of a powerful restraining force becomes an additional strong driving force in the direction of change.

Driving forces (Best Practices) that can help to create a more open and welcoming environment for adult learners might include support from one or more departments whose faculty involve adult learners in departmental curricula planning processes and decision making. In addition, these departments can relate learning outcomes and course assignments to the needs and circumstances of these learners. Other positive forces might include a prior learning assessment* process for experienced adult learners and the provision of information and counselling in various off-campus community locations, including workplaces, at times that are convenient for the learners.

Restraining forces might include lack of formal acknowledgement in the institution's mission statement of respect for adult learners and the legitimacy of their learning needs. Other forces working against a more open approach to serving adult learners might include limited access to institutional support services at times convenient for the learners, lack of flexible course delivery options, and course content that is not relevant to their life/work needs.

Figure 12-1 aims to demonstrate the applicability of Lewin's Force Field Analysis in relation to all eight of the key *Principles of Effectiveness* resulting from the CAEL Benchmarking Study. However, the Force Field model may also be used by you and your team to determine the driving and restraining forces for each of the key *Principles of Effectiveness* separately.

A list of selected readings on organizational change processes and work teams can be found at the end of Chapter 2. We hope that this resource material will be of use to you if you wish to explore these two areas in more depth.

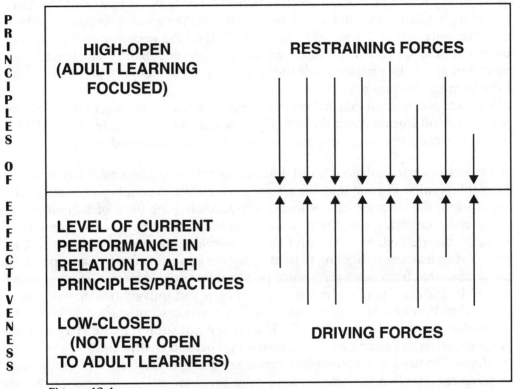

Figure 12-1

Critical Factors Needed for Success

Expanding your institution's reach and improvement on behalf of adult learners is never easy. The colleges and universities profiled in this book and in the CAEL Benchmarking Study have worked diligently over many years to reach the levels of excellence now recognized by so many others.

As you embark on the journey to move your institution closer to the operating principles of an Adult Learning Focused Institution, be mindful of both the assets and challenges you may face in the future. In the last section we applied the model of the Force Field Analysis to the Principles of Effectiveness, suggesting that an equilibrium is reached when the set of driving forces and restraining forces that intertwine and act collectively upon the Principles in Action are in balance. In this section we revisit the concept of the "critical success factors"—that is, the conditions or circumstances that presage success or failure—to suggest why the processes described in this workbook will lead directly to improved services for adult learners—or may end up sidetracked by issues or inaction. Thus, these critical success factors may be viewed as the actual embodiment of the driving or restraining forces within your institution.

The critical success factors we identify below may already be present as positive forces in your institutional environment. If so, then with proper and timely intervention on your part, the activities in this workbook may yield prompt and pleasing outcomes. However, it is the rare institution that will have all these factors weighed in favor of making changes in the directions we suggest. When, in fact, all the factors are present, chances are that the institution has already moved to a place that has forced it to become either bold or desperate—it can be unsettling to be in such environments where change occurs too readily! In reality, few colleges and universities are either bold or desperate; most are highly resistant to change. The implication here is that among these factors, you may find only a few working in your favor.

Regarding these critical success factors, we have no magic number or secret combination of ingredients to convey with a promise of success. Some factors may assume greater importance than other factors in a given situation, but which ones will have the greatest impact at your institution is something that only you and your colleagues can judge. We urge you to be thinking not only about your vision of what your institution can accomplish on behalf of its current and potential adult learners, but also to be realistic about the leverage you can obtain with the assets at your disposal and the barriers that you may face.

The critical factors discussed here fall into two groups: those pertaining to the *unmet need* (in this case, the needs of adult learners) and the *organizational factors* that facilitate or inhibit change.

Institutions are ready to change when an *unmet need* is demonstrated and is:

❖ *Consequential*—First, the need must be measurable and successful solutions must have observable results. Beyond that, the results must matter to people who matter. Within higher education, the simplest case is found in addressing the need of half-empty classrooms and the most satisfying result is succeeding in filling the empty seats. Some needs are not so readily ascertained, however, and their observable impact may be indirect rather than direct. Adult learners struggling to finance higher education are a case in point: their needs may be obscured from open view, since personal financial information is regarded as confidential. In addition, many who work for colleges and universities may regard paying for higher education as a mere administrative act, a precursor regarded as less consequential than students' academic performance. **The critical question for you: Why will it matter for your institution to become an Adult Learning Focused Institution?**

❖ *Persistent*—The need is not temporary and is not going to fix itself. The cheapest solution to any transient problem is to do nothing—the problem just goes away of its own accord. Returning to the example just given above, some institutions felt an enrollment pinch when the supply of secondary school graduates dropped (as it did in the U.S. for much of the 1990s). Demographers predicted a resurgence of secondary school graduates late in the 1990s, mitigating the problem (at least in part). Yet today many institutions still struggle to expand the pool of potential applicants—of all ages—because the landscape of student decision-making about higher education enrollment has changed considerably. **The critical question for you: Will the need to make yours an Adult Learning Focused Institution be transitory or sustained?**

❖ *Understood by Stakeholders*—One's understanding of a situation may be a function of one's proximity to or perspective upon the problem. To an instructor, a half-empty classroom might signify high potential for a quality learning experience; after all, it is thereby easier to get to know the students individually and to manage the class. However, the same half-empty classroom may signify under-utilization of expensive resources to the deans, administrators, and government officials who must fund the higher education enterprise. One of the most important elements in a successful change process is to identify fully and correctly *all* of the stakeholders in a given problem. In the context of adult learners in higher education, the sometimes 'forgotten' stakeholders include learners' families, employers or other sponsors, and communities. Failing to identify and involve all the relevant stakeholders may hamper the change effort. **The critical question for you: Are all of your key stakeholders committed to building an Adult Learning Focused Institution?**

❖ *Unresolved*—For some problems, stakeholders will readily admit, "Nothing is being done!" More often, though, somebody familiar with the problem will claim that "enough is being done," implying, "so let's move on to some other issue." The point here is that to influence change within an organization, it is not enough for the stakeholders to understand a given problem as consequential and persistent. Rather, they must come to believe that current and prior remedies have fallen short. In this respect, it is also not enough to have the data about a consequential and persistent problem in front of the stakeholders; there must be an interpretation of the data indicative of a failure. An important task of a change leader within an organization is to discredit, in an appropriate way, the weak and ineffectual remedies to significant problems, and this effort may be discouraged by those ready to argue that more time must be allowed to see what results the current remedies may bring. Until its failures are admitted, the organization might not be ready to try something new. **The critical question for you: Are past or current steps taken to build your Adult Learning Focused Institution viewed as insufficient?**

❖ *Urgent*—Change is difficult and often worrisome, while the routine and familiar feels comforting. Fears arise that new ways of working may, in fact, not work at all or at least not as well as the old way of doing things. Accordingly, a common inclination is to postpone dealing with unmet needs until they loom so large that they are unavoidable. Nonetheless, it is wiser to act while a problem is in its infancy, rather than after the crisis grows to catastrophic proportions. A key job of organizational leaders is to build consensus among stakeholders that past remedies to persistent and important unmet needs have not only failed, but that the time to act is now, not later—right now! **The critical question for you: Is improving your institution for adult learners an urgent issue?**

Institutions are also ready to change when certain organizational factors are present, such as:

❖ *Leadership*—Key leaders must champion the efforts to bring about improvements. Leadership roles come in many varieties, of course, and sometimes (but not always) they may be consolidated in the performance of a single person (who may or may not be the chief executive). *Opinion leaders* (who may be among the 'rank and file') influence the process by shaping shared perceptions and beliefs. *Authority figures* control important work systems, policies, and procedures, or human/financial resources necessary to accomplish the goals of an initiative. *Social/emotional leaders* inspire others, not through power or persuasive talents but by elevating human sentiments through compassionate, spiritual, or other concerns. In the context of your institution, the critical question may be what kind of leadership exerts the most leverage. **The critical question for you: Is key leadership behind your effort to make yours an Adult Learning Focused Institution?**

❖ *Adaptability*—Complementing the role of the leader who inspires others to move forward, members of the organizational community must be sufficiently flexible to adapt. The barriers here may be structural, contextual, or attitudinal. Structural barriers may include restrictive policies that permit no alternative ways of action—instructors might be required to conduct classes only in institutionally owned facilities. Contextual barriers may be circumstantial—students and instructors might be eager to hold classes at a workplace convenient for the students, but there is simply no space in the vicinity even remotely suitable for that purpose. Attitudinal barriers are often most troublesome: people in the organization believe it inappropriate and illegitimate to make any changes. A useful strategy for surmounting such barriers may be to link your current efforts with other recent successful change initiatives—either directly, or by describing your efforts as analogous to them. **The critical question for you: Are your colleagues able to respond positively to the changes that are needed and proposed?**

❖ *Resources*—A change initiative takes both time and money. When people are stretched to the limit by their current job duties and responsibilities, or when institutional revenues and budgets are severely constrained, or both, then the likelihood for starting something new is small. Here is where the connection to institutional leadership may be critical: persons in authority may need to free up the time or money necessary for those involved in the change effort you envision. Yet sometimes the resources are in the experiential domain: change efforts may require 'outside' points of view, bringing imagination and new concepts into context. In these latter circumstances, it is often extremely useful to bring external consultants into the institution for the purpose of sharing their experience in the service of the long-term goal of building internal capacities. **The critical question for you: Does the institution have the resources to sustain the change effort?**

❖ *Shared Values*—Moving a group of people towards a common end requires sufficient trust and communication that enables coordinated action to be possible. In organizations with strong internal coherence, many will view the organization's mission statement as defining the shared values of the people who work for it. In a university setting, though, it is not uncommon to find multiple missions: instruction, research, and service. If the emphasis is on instruction, "Students First" may represent the highest value. If the emphasis is on research, the highest value may be discovering and disseminating Truth. If service predominates, then collaboration and community involvement may reign. While not wholly incompatible, these three missions reflect very distinct orientations. Accordingly, appealing to the values implicit in a "Students First" approach may fail to excite those with a research agenda, whose fidelity is to the values inherent in creating and disseminating knowledge. **The critical question for you: Where do value orientations intersect within your institution to make the change process begin and to sustain it?**

Although we call them "success factors," in the final analysis, as told in the reality of what has happened at any given institution, there are no absolute, unqualified successes—or unmitigated failures. Every institution will accumulate "lessons learned" through its experiences with initiatives for improvement. Today's high-performance, adult-serving institutions are not so much lucky or exceptionally capable as they are dedicated and disciplined in their approach to serving adults. Although we have introduced examples of institutional responses to particular ALFI Principles throughout this workbook, we have not yet told the story of how an institution can put it all together. That is, how does an institution address and integrate successfully a connected set of practices across all eight key *Principles of Effectiveness*? In the next chapter we shall tell three such stories.

References

Flint, Thomas A. and Associates. (1999). *Best Practices in Adult Learning: A CAEL/APQC Benchmarking Study*. Chicago: Council for Adult and Experiential Learning.

Chapter 13

Putting It All Together

Stories of Successful Integration of the Principles

In CAEL's early work on Adult Learning Focused Institutions, we reported in detail about the CAEL Benchmarking Study to identify best practices in high-performance, adult-serving institutions. Six such institutions were visited in 1999 and were profiled in CAEL's book, *Best Practices in Adult Learning: A CAEL/APQC Benchmarking Study*. Those six institutions are:

- ❖ Athabasca University, Alberta, Canada
- ❖ School of New Resources, College of New Rochelle, New Rochelle, New York
- ❖ School for New Learning, DePaul University, Chicago, Illinois
- ❖ Empire State College, State University of New York, Saratoga Springs, New York
- ❖ Marylhurst University, Marylhurst, Oregon
- ❖ Sinclair Community College, Dayton, Ohio

As noted in the book, while these institutions are exemplary, by no means are they exclusively the best places for adult learners in higher education. They are outstanding for having implemented best practices, but they are not alone in that regard. Moreover, each of the six institutions CAEL visited had identified ongoing issues and challenges that they felt they still needed to master. Far from being viewed by the CAEL study team as a sign of weakness, these admissions of continuing challenge indicated to CAEL that each institution was still involved in continuous quality improvement—hence, they were likely to remain as leaders of innovative, adult-focused best practices.

Throughout earlier chapters we have described specific practices at select institutions that illustrate each Principle in action. However, we have yet to tackle the question: What does a fully integrated set of best practices look like at an Adult Learning Focused Institution? To answer this question necessitates telling a story about the institution as a whole. There are several good examples to refer to that precede the ALFI project. Perhaps the best-known adult-centered institution in the U.S. is the University of Phoenix, which as early as 1973 crafted a model for delivery of educational programming that has been adopted by dozens of institutions. The founders of the University of Phoenix, John Sperling and Robert W. Tucker, have detailed key features of this model in a recent book, *The University of Phoenix: A Model for an Adult-Centered Professional University* (Sperling & Tucker, 1997). Not surprisingly, several elements of that model, as detailed by these authors, resonate with the Principles of Effectiveness that flow out of the ALFI project. Among the elements of the model are:

- ❖ Students as change agents, tapping their experience and practical focus;
- ❖ Faculty as learning facilitators, carefully selected and trained for that role;
- ❖ Curriculum as a repository for best practices, subject to continuous improvement;
- ❖ Structure and governance in which accountability and effectiveness are rewarded;

❖ Quality management through surveying of multiple stakeholders; and

❖ Adult learning outcomes assessment as key to the enterprise.

(Sperling and Tucker, 1997)

We highly recommend further study of this model by all those who are interested in improving institutions for adult learners. The founders of the University of Phoenix demonstrate that they understand why the institution-wide integration of adult-focused practices is necessary in order to be effective. In their words, "Students learn not only from the curriculum and faculty, but also from the infrastructure formed by the principles that guide the selection of faculty, the creation of the curricula, and the provision of educational support services" (Sperling & Tucker, 1997, p. 90).

The University of Phoenix is not alone in this regard. Useful profiles of thirty other adult-serving institutions can be found in Maehl (2000), and a book-length treatment of the formula for effectiveness used by the Community College of Denver has also recently been published (Roueche, Ely, and Roueche, 2001). While we recommend these to readers for their valuable insights, none of them necessarily includes all of the elements that the ALFI project has identified as critical, including best practices surrounding the Financing, Life & Career Planning, and Technology Principles, for example. Accordingly, we wish to tell some stories of institutions that successfully integrate their educational services from the perspective of the eight Principles we have presented here.

Below, we profile three additional institutions: a community college, an upper-division public university, and a private university. We tell their stories as being noteworthy of their continuing efforts to fulfill their missions in the spirit of the Adult Learning Focused Institution, long before this initiative was organized by CAEL. Each of these institutions was visited by one or more of the co-authors of this workbook. We identify their strengths, using the framework of the eight key *Principles of Effectiveness*, even though their accomplishments took root long before the worksheets herein were developed. Like the six institutions in the original benchmarking study, each of these institutions is ready to acknowledge their unresolved challenges, but like those same six, their effort to improve is continuous.

Board of Governors Degree Program
Governors State University (University Park, Illinois)

(Paul Zakos and Ruth Frey prepared the following profile after their visit to Governors State University on December 7, 2000. For more information, visit http://www.govst.edu.)

Background

Governors State University (GSU), located outside the Chicago metropolitan area, is a public degree-completion university serving more than 9,000 juniors, seniors, and master's degree students. GSU offers one of the largest non-traditional Bachelor of Arts degree programs in Illinois. Called the "Board of Governors" (BOG) Program, it is flexible and student-oriented, allowing adults to work with an advisor to design a B.A. in Liberal Studies. The BOG program is offered at more than 30 off-campus sites, and via several technology-based instructional tools such as telecourses or instruction over the Internet.

The average age of all students at GSU is 35 (the average age of Board of Governors B.A. Program is 40). More than 70 percent of students at GSU are women, many of whom work, raise families, and take advantage of the child care provided on campus. Eighty percent of the institution's non-traditional students attend the university part time, with 44 percent receiving financial aid.

Outreach

> The institution conducts its outreach to adult learners by overcoming barriers of time, place, and tradition in order to create lifelong access to educational opportunities.

The first contact with potential adult enrollees in the Board of Governors (BOG) program is in the pre-enrollment phase, which marks the beginning of what the BOG professional advisors hope will be a long-term relationship with the adult learner. One of the stated aims of the BOG's outreach to adult learners is to create a "learning community locally and across the country to help adult learners achieve their goals." A great deal of time is given in the pre-advising sessions to describing the flexibility of course selection and degree composition, and to explain the variety of choices available to adults in designing their own degrees. Every student must have an advising interview during the first semester in the BOG Program.

The BOG staff and faculty make a concerted effort to reach and sustain adult learners though dialogue—though this "dialogue" need not necessarily begin with face-to-face conversation. For example, the BOG Program has developed a 48-minute, pre-admission video that begins with a welcome by the Academic Program's Director. On the tape, four advisors discuss frequently asked questions about the BOG Program, compiled from the comments/queries of previous adult students. The advisors each discuss the various academic and personal challenges presented by the Program and they encourage learners to reflect upon their reasons for wanting to enter the Program to pursue a degree. The advisors also make it clear that they expect adult learners to take a great deal of responsibility for their own learning and for customizing their course work to fit their own needs, circumstances, and goals. The advisors clearly state that they are available to assist adult learners to make the decision about whether to enroll at GSU, and they encourage them to contact one of the advisors in the BOG Program if they have any questions related to enrollment.

BOG staff understand the importance of helping adult learners make well-informed decisions about pursuing a degree at the University, and they make a concerted effort to ensure that all of their questions are answered clearly and accurately prior to enrollment. The aforementioned video describes the BOG Prior Learning Assessment (PLA) option, which involves having qualified candidates complete portfolios to gain experiential learning credits for University courses. The advisors also describe the supports available to learners who may need help with writing, mathematics, and other subjects, and they outline the variety of course delivery methods available to adult learners.

The pre-admission videotape is indicative of—but does not exclusively define—the University's willingness to innovate to meet adult learners' needs and preferences. Consider the intriguing project the University recently undertook with assistance from the Fund for the Improvement of Post-Secondary Education. The project, called ABE-LINC, permitted students to enroll simultaneously in one of fifteen participating community colleges and the University, completing their degree work at the University via distance learning. Thus, unlike the traditional approach in which the student is expected to first complete an associate degree at a community college, then later apply and enroll at the university level for the bachelor's degree, the ABE-LINC program permitted the student to begin and do both simultaneously.

Life and Career Planning

> The institution addresses the adult learner's life and career goals before or at the onset of enrollment in order to assess and align its capacities to help learners reach their goals.

In addition to the pre-admission video mentioned above, the University further engages newly enrolled adult learners in a dialogue about their goals via a questionnaire that is included with a cover letter from the Director of the BOG Program, congratulating them upon acceptance of their enrollment. The questionnaire consists of seven areas designed to help adult learners reflect on their experiences as learners, their hopes for the future, and the ways in which the University can help them achieve their learning goals. Adult learners are advised to be as brief or as detailed as they wish in answering the questions. They are encouraged to send completed questionnaires to their advisors by fax, e-mail, or regular mail prior to the first meeting with their advisor.

The questionnaire provides a basic framework for the important, continuing dialogue between adult learners and BOG advisors. It also encourages and supports adult learners to think critically about their decision to return to formal study. It helps the adult learner to begin to examine in detail the specific terminology, structures, processes, requirements, and demands that will be made upon them as students. The "frequently asked questions" portion of the questionnaire focuses on critical areas such as the length of time it may take to finish the degree, important admissions criteria, prerequisites for specific courses, and the steps involved in the preparation of a PLA portfolio for college-level prior learning credits.

In addition to the letter from the Director, adult learners receive a congratulatory letter from their advisor that updates them on their current status at the University, vis-à-vis issues such as academic transcripts from other institutions, and any other materials forwarded to the University as part of the admissions process. The advisor's letter tends to reinforce the basic information contained in the Director's letter. In addition, the advisor's letter reminds the learner of other important processes and policies such as the compulsory basic writing and math proficiency exams, the minimum requirements for an acceptable grade point average, and the process for initiating a request for academic credits for prior learning.

BOG advisors assist adult learners in making important decisions primarily on a one-to-one basis by helping them develop initial study plans. They also work with learners to focus their energies on the competencies they wish to obtain while in the Program and the courses needed to achieve them.

Taken together, these communiqués welcome adult learners and quickly and systematically introduce them to critical tasks and processes related to study at GSU, including the steps necessary to arrange for an important first meeting with their advisor. For those adults living at a distance from the University, the option of having the first advising session by telephone is available. Regardless of the means by which it is done, the advising process of the BOG program is ongoing and intensive.

One of the strengths of the BOG Program is its flexibility. Adult learners have the opportunity to take courses in a variety of disciplines. This diversity enables learners to sample from a variety of subjects and disciplines, which may be crucial if the learner is not yet clear on a career direction.

Financing

The institution promotes choice using an array of payment options for adult learners in order to expand equity and financial flexibility.

The BOG Program has among the lowest tuition rates and student fees ($110 per credit hour, including the student activity fee) in the State of Illinois. Adult learners are able to pay an hourly fee for courses, rather than the traditional full tuition rate. If students decide to take a maximum of fifteen or sixteen credit hours in a semester, they are only required to pay a total that is equivalent to twelve hours. The University's board of trustees has pledged that tuition increases will not exceed the U.S. Consumer Price Index plus three percent in any given school year, for a period of five consecutive years. True to the standard for accredited institutions, adult learners wishing to withdraw or drop courses are eligible for tuition refunds ranging from one hundred to fifty percent of the fees, depending upon date of withdrawal.

The BOG Program has an installment payment option for students which requires a payment of fifty percent of the total fees at the beginning of the semester, with the balance being paid at the end of the term. The BOG Program also enters into third party financial agreements with employers, in order to free the student from being caught between the University's bills and their employers' sponsorship payments. Two examples of such arrangements occur with the State of Illinois, in its Upward Mobility Program, and with the United Parcel Service (UPS). In both instances, tuition payments are sent by employers at the end of each course, with the payments going directly to the University's business office.

The University actively promotes financing equity for adult learners. Traditionally, financial assistance from government sources has not been available to students taking only one course (three to four credit hours). Fortunately, the Illinois Student Assistance Commission (ISAC) awards eligible state residents a need-based Monetary Award Program (MAP) grant. Due in part to strong lobbying by the University, MAP awards have now been extended to students who enroll for less than six credit hours (the previous eligibility threshold). The University lobbied strongly with the Illinois State Legislature and the Illinois Board of Higher Education to extend this Program to part-time students because of the importance of adult learners to the well being of the state's economic future.

Yet, the University does not rely exclusively upon outside financing for students taking only one course at a time. Unlike many other universities that heap financial assistance only upon full-time students, Governors State University makes provisions from its own institutional resources for financial assistance to these "very part-time" students. The GSU Foundation and the GSU Alumni Association sponsor the Learning Excellence Award for Persisters (LEAP) which provides monetary awards to students who are enrolled for less than six hours per semester. Also, the Public Service Scholarship Program is available for employees in the public service sector who are taking five credit hours or less. These awards are designed for those students whose life circumstances might hinder their ability to continue working toward a degree on a part-time basis while juggling all of their other life responsibilities. Funds for this program have been established by a private anonymous donor and are made available to students as grants rather than loans. The Financial Aid Office at the University actively seeks out adult learners who may be eligible for these awards.

Adult learners are also welcome to apply for regular financial aid awards. Financial advising is available throughout each weekday and the Financial Aid Office is also open four evenings per week, with a cashier available two evenings per week. Since all of the University's BOG students are students who have transferred from other institutions (where they may have received financial aid), the financial aid offered by the University is often coordinated between the University and its several partner institutions, which are most commonly community colleges.

Assessment of Learning Outcomes

> The institution defines and assesses the knowledge, skills, and competencies
> acquired by adult learners both from the curriculum and from life/work experience
> in order to assign credit and confer degrees with rigor.

University faculty members are required to develop program and course learning outcomes for all of their credit courses at the University. Faculty members are also required to participate in ongoing professional development activities that touch on a variety of topics, including multiple assessment techniques. The University Curriculum Committee and the University Assessment Committee collaboratively determine whether all courses offered at GSU fit their standard syllabus format, which includes competency statements and appropriate defining terminology.

The BOG program has a well-established Prior Learning Assessment (PLA) program that enables adult learners to gain credit for learning that is at the level of higher education, toward the requirements of a Bachelor of Arts degree. Portfolios are assessed by University faculty and/or external experts, who make final decisions on credit awards. The BOG office also helps other departments at the University evaluate experiential learning for academic credit for adult learners enrolled in other bachelor's degree programs. Adult learners interested in pursuing Credit through Evaluation of Experiential Learning (CEEL) for any university degree program are encouraged to contact their specific program advisors about completing a PLA portfolio.

A non-credit PLA seminar is offered twice per year to help learners develop portfolios. Print and videotape resource materials are also available to assist learners who may not be able to attend the seminar. GSU and several partner institutions are producing an online version of this seminar to be delivered for elective credit via the Internet. These resources provide a systematic, step-by-step process for constructing portfolios for academic credit. Beyond the residency requirement which dictates that learners must take a minimum of twenty-four credit hours at the University, the remaining credit hours are eligible for PLA credit for qualified candidates.

Employers often approach the University with workplace-based education and training needs, and the University willingly enters into discussions with them to help meet those needs. For example, the criminal justice program has a high number of adult learners enrolled in the program from a wide variety of services, including corrections, human resources, and mental health. Courses are offered throughout the community and at a variety of sites, some of which include the Cook County Jail and St. James Hospital. The PLA Portfolio Development process is widely used in the criminal justice program. This program also has a senior student seminar that focuses on the assessment of exit program outcomes, career development, the creation of a resume, and an oral examination.

Teaching-Learning Process

> The institution's faculty use multiple methods of instruction (including experiential and problem-based methods) for adult learners in order to connect curricular concepts to useful knowledge and skills.

Whenever possible, faculty members utilize a variety of instructional approaches that incorporate the tasks, issues, symbols and language of the adult learner in the context of both the community and the workplace. For example, the criminal justice program offers many of its courses at a variety of community-based corrections settings in response to the needs of adult learners who are pursuing degrees in criminal justice. Full- and part-time faculty members deliver these courses, and they travel to community-based sites to provide courses at times convenient for the learners (often as part of their regular teaching loads). This strong connection to community and workplaces benefits curriculum development, too. The criminal justice program has recently begun to plan for the implementation of a new specialty in the area of computer crime. This need was uncovered, in part, through the University's interaction with adult learners and their employers in the criminal justice system, as a response to the increasing use of computers for illegal purposes.

Faculty members at the University employ a variety of teaching methods, ranging from group projects to quality circles and learner-led activities, depending upon the particular discipline being studied. The average class size for adult learners is seventeen, and some classes have as few as eight students. GSU has an extensive experiential learning component that takes many different forms—clinical and skill placements, internships, and similar approaches, which vary according to discipline. The University has contracts with every type of organization in its region, also based on the particular disciplines being studied.

The fact that the BOG program does not have an institutionally defined major area of study allows adult learners to pursue specific areas in a wide variety of subjects and disciplines, thereby enabling them to design their own majors based on interests and needs. This individualized approach permits adult learners to create optimal connections to their practical concerns as well as their life/career goals. The additional focus of study within the BOG program is within academic minors, and there are approximately nineteen areas from which to choose, depending on the learner's interests.

The University utilizes a combination of full-time tenured faculty and part-time adjunct faculty, plus multiple methods of instructional delivery to respond to learner needs on-campus and in a variety of community-based settings. Part-time instructors use the same learning resource materials (syllabi, learning modules, and learning outcomes) as full-time faculty. A wide array of credit courses is offered via audiotape, television/videotapes, correspondence, CD-ROMs, and Web-based options, as well as the more traditional lecture format. Some full-time faculty members who teach adults in off-campus settings rarely visit the institution, except to attend staff meetings. Part-time faculty members are often drawn from community-based professions such as medicine, criminal justice, and human services because of their professional training and experience in the field.

Student Support Systems

> The institution assists adult learners using comprehensive academic and student support systems to enhance students' capacities to become self-directed, lifelong learners.

The University recognizes the importance of providing academic and student support services to adult learners as soon as possible after they make the initial inquiry at the institution. For example, prospective students receive a 48-minute videotape that introduces important questions about students' goals and aspirations. Among the questions raised are: Why are you interested in pursuing a degree? How long are you prepared to spend at this effort? What are your personal strengths and weaknesses?

In addition to the welcome letter from the Director of the Program and an assigned Academic Advisor sent to newly-admitted students, new enrollees must also have an initial interview with their advisor as soon as possible (within a month) after they register at the University. Advisors are drawn from each academic discipline, and many adult learners have faculty mentors as well. Advisors play key roles in helping to ensure that adult learners are taking the courses they need in the appropriate discipline. Career counselors are also available to help adults make important choices by using a variety of tests and providing ongoing support and counseling.

Having established early initial contact with adult learners upon their entry to the University, advisors maintain ongoing contact with learners throughout their stay in order to monitor their changing needs, goals, and life circumstances. Letters are sent to all adult learners reminding them of the importance of having periodic assessments to determine their progress towards achieving their goals. As adult learners get close to finishing their degrees, advisors help them prepare the necessary documentation (e.g., transcripts, correct course selections) needed to graduate.

Early advising and counseling does not, of course, substitute for assessments and support that are essential to do the academic work of an institution of higher education. All students studying to complete a bachelor's degree must take proficiency/standardized competency exams. All undergraduate degree-seeking students must attempt the Arithmetic Skills, Elementary Algebra and Conventions of Written English Proficiency exams during their first semester at the University. The University offers online help with writing assignments through its web site. Support is provided for proficiency tests, questions about problems with writing, referrals to resources to help improve writing skills, and feedback on writing samples. The University's Center for Learning Assistance helps learners to improve their math skills and offers math tutorials online.

GSU is one of the rare institutions that has successfully addressed the difficult issue of child care support that many adult learners need. The University's Child Care Center offers services to parents with children from three to twelve years of age. Parents have several different program options from which to choose, such as day care, evening-hours care, summer camp, before- and after-school programs, and drop-in care.

Technology

> The institution uses information technology to provide relevant and timely information and to enhance the learning experience.

Adult learners interested in enrolling and studying at the University have a variety of program registration and course delivery options. For example, they may initiate the formal registration process either in-person, by touch-tone telephone, or by e-mail. The University provides credit-bearing, technology-enriched courses for adult learners who need to be able to organize their learning around family, work, and community obligations. The University also offers a wide array of correspondence and Internet-based credit courses, in addition to producing and delivering television and videotaped courses. The University acknowledges the importance of sculpting course delivery around the times, places, and schedules of adult learners. Thus, the University is able to deliver credit courses throughout the State of Illinois—and across the country—in a variety of flexible, timely, and convenient formats, suited to the lives of busy adults.

The University operates a cable television station on campus. At any one time, some 45 to 60 sites in the campus area deliver a variety of courses, either through the interactive video network or the other outreach programs. Instructional videotapes purchased from the University bookstore can be returned each trimester during "book buy-back weeks," and learners can receive a refund of up to fifty percent of the original price of the videotape(s).

The University plans to offer as many of its programs as possible online, in order to serve a higher number of adult learners more efficiently. As part of this expansion process, the University is keenly aware of the importance of making sure that important academic and personal support services such as financial aid, library resources, and career counseling are also available online.

Strategic Partnerships

> The institution engages in strategic relationships, partnerships, and collaborations with employers and other organizations to develop and improve educational opportunities for adult learners.

Governors State University was created in large part to respond to external community needs. For example, the Children and Family Service option has been offered at GSU for the past five years because no other state-supported universities were willing to offer credit courses to employed human service workers on a part-time, evening basis.

The University is constantly striving to work more closely with employers in both the public and private sectors to meet employees' skill and knowledge needs. The University is open to delivering courses either at the work-site or nearby in the local community, if possible. Examples of such efforts include:

❖ The University is currently negotiating with St. James Hospital to provide on-site in-service training for both credit and non-credit activities.
❖ The University's Public Administration Program offers on-site classes in downtown Chicago for employees of the State of Illinois.
❖ The College of Education works closely with regional school districts to meet the needs of students, administrators, and educators.

❖ The University has recently obtained government funding to collaboratively build a training center in partnership with the Ford Motor Company, local community schools and Prairie State College. One of the training needs that will be met by this effort will be to help newly hired employees at the Ford Motor Company plant to become computer literate, so that they can function effectively on the production line in the assembly plant.

Brevard Community College—Melbourne Campus (Melbourne, Florida)

(Paul Zakos and Ruth Frey prepared the following profile after their visit to Brevard Community College on February 7, 2001. For more information, visit http://www.brevard.cc.fl.us.)

Background

The Melbourne Campus of Brevard Community College (BCC) opened in 1971 and is one of four campuses that serve Brevard County, Florida. The campus serves approximately 45 percent of the college-wide enrollment and the average age of students is 29. Melbourne Campus provides students with flexible class scheduling, including day and evening courses as well as a Weekend College, an accelerated and concentrated learning program that offers the opportunity to complete an entire Associate in Arts degree program through weekend classes in less than two years. The College equips students for upper division baccalaureate studies, and technical and vocational programs that lead to the following degrees: Associate in Arts, Associate in Science, and Postsecondary Vocational Certificate. In 1987 Brevard was honored with the Institutional Service Award from CAEL.

Outreach

> The institution conducts its outreach to adult learners overcoming barriers of time, place, and tradition in order to create lifelong access to educational opportunities.

The educational process is traditionally viewed as courses comprising subject matter, acquired on campus and based on seat time. At Brevard Community College, effective outreach to adult learners means viewing education as learning comprised of competencies, acquired anywhere and based on experience. Several distinctive features of Brevard Community College speak to this inclusive vision of what higher education can be.

Brevard does not wait for prospective students to come to its campuses. Recently, the College conducted a marketing effort targeted towards employed adult learners through the use of contacts at fifty of the most important employers in the area. Brevard mailed information packages to human resource departments and then made follow-up telephone calls in order to advise these companies of the services available at Brevard, and to offer to hold classes at the workplace. In addition, BCC conducts outreach to adult learners through the clergy and various other religious institutions serving minority populations in the area.

At Brevard, the advising process begins before the adult learner formally enrolls. Student development specialists and admissions staff answer as many questions as possible to help prospective adult learners deal with important questions related to their career goals and personal aspirations. Admissions staff members make a concerted effort to answer questions of prospective learners immediately, rather than sending the potential students away only to have them return for a second or third appointment. The college makes the admissions process as painless as possible, and does so by acknowledging that many adults return to formal study with fear and trepidation, and often in response to significant transitions which seriously affect their family, community, and/or employment status. Brevard has one central location which houses admissions, financial aid, student advisors, and its career center.

Faculty members play many different, non-traditional roles at Brevard. An illuminating example of the innovative involvement of Brevard faculty with adult learners occurs in the College's Service Learning Program. Approximately one hundred and ten faculty per semester are actively engaged in Service Learning projects, involving close to 3,000 students, many of whom are adult learners. Faculty members are able to enrich course content, instructional delivery, and the practical application of theory through a wide range of community-based Service Learning projects. Importantly, the Brevard faculty members are allowed to participate in service learning projects for their own personal learning, as well.

Life and Career Planning

> The institution addresses adult learners' life and career goals before or at the onset of enrollment in order to assess and align its capacities to help learners reach their goals.

All incoming Brevard students must participate in a mandatory student orientation process, which occurs in the student's first semester. Learners who participate successfully in the course called "Success Strategies for College and Life," are exempted from further orientation requirements, and they also receive three credits for the course. Through this induction to Brevard, program advisors provide ongoing counselling and personal support services for adult learners who need help in making important decisions which affect their personal and career goals.

Brevard's Career Resources Center provides a wide array of resources designed to help adult learners define their education and career goals and to develop realistic educational plans to achieve these goals. The Career Center offers workshops on job search techniques, and career exploration opportunities via internships, co-ops, and job shadowing. In addition, there are several print and computerized resources (including web-sites and software packages) designed to help adult learners assess their own skills, interests, and preferences related to specific areas of employment, further study and scholarship (financial aid) opportunities. The Center also provides ongoing, one-on-one counseling that focuses on identifying individual strengths and opportunities for the continued development of adult learners in meeting their personal and career goals.

A key means by which adult learners at Brevard become active partners in the planning, delivery and evaluation of their own learning is through the Center for Service Learning. The Center for Service Learning actively engages learners in a variety of meaningful, community-based learning experiences in which classroom theory is applied in a variety of real life settings. These learning opportunities are campus-wide and interspersed among a variety of departments and disciplines. Adult learners have a number of opportunities through the Center to acquire new skills and knowledge, and to put their existing skills and knowledge into practice in community and college-based projects that are related to the curriculum, their own interests and needs, and the needs of the community.

An important component of addressing adult learners' goals is the appropriate recognition and respect given to their prior learning achievements from life and work. Brevard provides several opportunities for adult learners to receive college credits for experiential learning acquired from work and other informal learning opportunities, such as volunteer activities, self-directed study, or military service. Such credits may be obtained via Credit by Examination, College Level Examination Program (CLEP), DANTES, credit for prior military training/education and Credit for Adult Experiential Learning, a BCC course that helps adult learners organize their experiential learning for college credit.

Financing

> The institution promotes choice using an array of payment options for adult learners in order to expand equity and financial flexibility.

Brevard recognizes that a first step to assuring access to higher education for adult learners is to keep education affordable. The cost per credit hour for courses taken by residents of Brevard County at BCC is $51.25—among the lowest of colleges and universities in the area. A second step is to assure convenience in payment processing. Adult learners can pay tuition fees online, by telephone, or in person. The cashier's office is open through the lunch hour and until 6:00 pm, Monday through Thursday. Deferred tuition payments are possible at BCC; they are handled on a case-by-case basis. Credit card payment is accepted for those who find it convenient.

Despite the low tuition rate, financial assistance is still a necessity for a substantial number of adult learners at Brevard. Advice about financial aid is available online, and forms can be downloaded, faxed, or handled in person at the College. The financial aid office helps adult learners to select financial assistance from among nine scholarship opportunities geared specifically for adult learners who are studying on a part time basis. Financial aid is also available for those learners participating in college preparatory courses at the same cost as credit courses.

Assessment of Learning Outcomes

> The institution defines and assesses the knowledge, skills, and competencies acquired by adult learners both from the curriculum and from life/work experience in order to assign credit and confer degrees with rigor.

Brevard Community College uses an outcomes-based approach for all of its credit courses. Thus, a prime focus is put upon learning achieved—not just material covered—in all credit courses. An institution-wide protocol is used to ensure that all course syllabi adhere to the same format in terms of how learning outcomes are identified and described.

With respect to Prior Learning Assessment (PLA), the College has a well-established PLA Portfolio Development credit course (Credit for Adult Experiential Learning), designed to help learners articulate, document, and obtain credit for college-level learning acquired outside of Brevard. This course can be taken online or in a regular classroom setting. Adult learners can obtain a maximum of sixteen out of a total of 60 to 68 credits through the PLA process, depending upon their degree goals. Mentoring and ongoing advising are two of the important functions performed by the portfolio course instructor in helping adult learners to identify and articulate their learning as it may relate to their education and career plans.

The College has also developed a separate, stand-alone Community Service Center curriculum that integrates community service and academic theory more directly. This curriculum design enables adult learners and community-based organizations to identify the skills and knowledge needed for competent, caring, community service. Brevard makes an ongoing effort to consult with a variety of stakeholder groups, including businesses, industry groups, and community service organizations, to ensure that their education and training needs are addressed by the College.

Teaching-Learning Process

> The institution's faculty use multiple methods of instruction (including experiential and problem-based methods) for adult learners in order to connect curricular concepts to useful knowledge and skills.

Brevard Community College's Service Learning Program utilizes a teaching-learning process that involves a high degree of interaction and participation among learners, faculty, and the community. Service Learning integrates academic theory with practical, hands-on experience in a variety of community-based settings ranging from health care to literacy to the environment. The Center for Service Learning provides recruitment, placement and support. It matches the interests/needs of the learner and the community by integrating them with a variety of academic programs and courses across the college. Faculty members help to integrate service learning into more than one hundred and twenty courses at Brevard, involving thousands of students in more than 300 course sections.

As a result of the Service Learning process, faculty are better able to help learners relate course content and concepts to the learner's own life experiences and to community-based needs. Self-assessment is a major component of the Service Learning Program. Learners are required to maintain reflective journals that enable them to analyze, strengthen, guide, and document important learning (skills, knowledge and attitudes) which are developed and enhanced as a result of their community service experience. The learning that results from this reflective process is often directly related to learning objectives and course outcomes. Many adult learners utilize service learning to build upon existing skills and knowledge and/or to branch out into entirely new career and personal learning opportunities.

The college's senior administration encourages faculty members to participate in service learning, too. Faculty are offered incentives such as resource materials to assist them with reflection and assessment processes, sabbaticals for service learning research and program development, and special grants to support curriculum modification. Service Learning forms part of new faculty orientation sessions, and faculty involvement in Service Learning is taken into account in tenure and promotional decisions.

In addition to the Service Learning Program, Brevard's Cooperative Education Program also relates classroom study to supervised practical experience in a variety of settings in business, industry, government, and community services. To the maximum extent possible, the Cooperative Education Program integrates academic and career goals with program objectives in a variety of disciplines.

Adult learners have several methods of course and program delivery options from which to choose at Brevard Community College, including televised, web based, Weekend College, and independent study. Brevard offers a variety of credit courses by television through its own TV station (WBCC) and regional cable systems. Courses are offered twice per week, and Brevard offers an orientation to TV learning via videotape. Video copies of the orientation to TV learning, and all courses, are available for use at each campus library. Texts and other resource materials are also available at the campus bookstore.

BCC On-Line, at http://www.brevard.cc.fl.us, is Brevard's virtual campus. It offers adult learners all of the support services available on the conventional campus. Besides its instructional activities, the virtual campus enables learners to apply for admissions, register for classes, receive academic advising, apply for financial aid, and use the library, all online.

Brevard's Weekend College offers a variety of credit courses to meet General Education requirements for upper division academic preparation, as well as for course electives in education and business. In the Weekend College, course offerings are more intensive and concentrated than traditional programs. Classes (terms) are held on twelve consecutive weekends. Learners typically enroll in three courses, earning nine semester credit hours in each of seven terms. PLA credits enable qualified students attending Weekend College to finish the degree program in less than two years. Faculty members who teach in the Weekend College are drawn from among those who teach in BCC's regular semester systems.

Brevard's Independent Study option enables adult learners to take courses through independent study. With the use of this option, adult learners are able to meet course requirements on an individualized basis by meeting with faculty and developing a plan to complete course requirements.

Student Support Systems

> The institution assists adult learners using comprehensive academic and support systems in order to enhance students' capabilities to become self-directed, life-long learners.

Adult learners predominate at Brevard Community College, and the College has geared itself accordingly. The average age of learners at Brevard is 29, and sixty percent of the student population enroll as part-time students who average between seven and eight credits per semester (a full-time study program consists of twelve or more credits). Sixty percent of these part-time students are female and Brevard provides child care in the evenings so that parents wishing to enroll in evening courses may bring their children with them. Since many students take Brevard's courses at the workplace, the College may provide support services there, too. For example, there is a small campus at the Kennedy Space Center for adult learners who work either for National Aeronautics and Space Administration (NASA) or for the variety of contractors who work at the Center. There, the College provides counseling and other support services along with course delivery.

Brevard recognizes the convenience of the "one-stop" approach to service. Brevard has recently renovated its student administrative offices so that the College may house all student services in one building. With the various support services located virtually next door to each other, Brevard minimizes the amount of time that adult learners spend obtaining the assistance they require.

Proper academic placement and/or preparation is part of Brevard's support system. As part of the admissions process, all degree-seeking students applying to Brevard for the first time must submit scores no more than two years old from state-approved placement tests. Test scores are used to assess skill levels in writing, reading and math to ensure placement in appropriate levels of academic study. Learners who do not meet minimum scores in one or more subject areas must successfully complete college-preparatory courses prior to enrolling in college credit courses. Learners who are not successful in preparatory courses are provided guidance in pursuing alternate methods of preparatory instruction.

The Career Center and Veterans Affairs Office provide ongoing career counseling and personal support for adult learners. A major goal of the Career Center is "to help adults successfully cope with the normal anxieties involved in returning to formal study." This includes helping them tap into existing support networks, identifying strengths, researching career options, contact with potential employers through co-op placements, etc. College staff, faculty advisors, and adult learners establish relationships prior to enrollment that continue while they are formally enrolled and often sustain themselves after graduation.

Brevard's Office of Veteran Affairs provides veterans a wide array of counseling and support services. The office helps veterans make important career and personal choices as quickly and efficiently as possible. As part of the admissions process, all incoming veterans participate in an academic assessment and goal-setting activity to assist them in developing an education/career plan. The Office of Veterans Affairs has also prepared a Veteran's Information Guide which summarizes key issues relating to admissions, financing, educational benefits, enrollment policies, grading, credit for military training, etc. The Guide enables veterans returning to formal study to quickly begin addressing the most important demands and responsibilities of formal study. Counselors provide needed support and advice in helping veterans to understand the conventions and processes of the College during the pre-admission phase, throughout enrollment, and often after graduation.

BCC works hard to create a sense of community among its adult learner population and tries to deal with the whole person by viewing advising and mentoring as key elements of its service to adult learners. Adult learners are treated with respect by staff and faculty, who help them review their personal and career options and strengthen their self-esteem. If adult learners experience difficulties, mentors drawn from faculty and staff across the college are often assigned to assist them in dealing with the challenges they face.

Effective communication is key to maintaining a supportive college community. Brevard communicates with adult learners and provides information, support, counseling, and course delivery in a variety of different formats. For example, college information is available on its web site, and interaction with learners often occurs via e-mail. College information/orientation sessions are offered online and on-site at the College, depending upon the needs of the learner. Faculty, staff, and administrators are available to provide information and advice to learners prior to and during enrollment.

Technology

> The institution uses information technology to provide relevant and timely information to enhance the learning experience.

Brevard uses a variety of information technologies to reach out to adult learners in order to provide them with information about the College and to deliver a variety of support and educational services, including credit courses. The College's web site is set up to handle requests for information about almost any aspect of the services provided at Brevard. Prospective students can e-mail their questions to college personnel or have them answered online. Financial aid applications are processed online, and the necessary financial aid forms can be downloaded or faxed to the college. The compulsory orientation to the college can be done either online or in person. Online courses enable adult learners to take all or part of their academic programs—including an Associate of Arts degree in General Studies, an Associate of Science degree in Legal Assisting, and five non-credit vocational certificate programs—in a highly individualized manner without setting foot on the campus.

Brevard has a Televised Interactive Education Service that links the College's four campuses, enabling courses to originate at any campus and to be received at the other campuses. Televised and web-based credit courses meet the same instructional objectives as regular in-class courses. The major differences between in-person and web-based courses are the delivery method and the amount of responsibility shouldered by the learner. An online bulletin board allows learners to communicate with instructors.

Brevard recently upgraded its Information Request Service System to include a special phone line/number for adult learners who may be interested in registering at the college. This number is linked with a new computer system, though which a staff member handles the incoming telephone call request, enters the information into the computer's database, and sends an information package immediately to the prospective student.

Strategic Partnerships

> The institution engages in strategic relationships, partnerships, and collaborations with employers and other organizations in order to develop and improve educational opportunities for adult learners.

Brevard reaches out in many ways to other organizations in order to provide education and training opportunities for adult learners. The College has several staff whose primary function is to contact representatives of business and industry, and to identify, coordinate, and deliver community- and workplace-based courses and programs. The Brevard Industry and Training Consortium employs a Director of Business and Industry Training whose job entails serving as liaison to business and industry, conducting county-wide needs assessments, and making referrals to any of the four Brevard campuses as appropriate. Whenever possible, the College helps adult learners gain college credit for specific industry-based training and assists them with enhancing their employability by providing courses related to the competencies required in their occupation. For example, Brevard has helped workers employed in the telecommunications industry to upgrade their qualifications, enabling them to receive higher rates of pay and job classifications.

BCC staff members regularly visit a variety of workplaces at the request of employers and as a part of the College's outreach strategy. The goal of this effort is to assist organizations and companies in meeting the changing knowledge and skill requirements of their incumbent workforce. In recent years, Brevard has developed a unique educational relationship with staff at the Kennedy Space Center. The College has worked closely with NASA and its educational department in order to coordinate NASA training needs with related courses and programs offered by Brevard. In addition to employees of NASA, the College offers courses to employees of contractors (such as the Boeing and Lockheed corporations) and to military personnel working on the site. Many of these federal contractors pay for tuition and books for their employees and offer special company incentives for successful completion of academic work. The PLA portfolio development program at Brevard has been a useful option for a variety of personnel employed at the Kennedy Space Center who are pursuing college diplomas.

The Service Learning and Cooperative Education Programs at BCC have developed collaborative relationships with well more than 300 organizations in Brevard County. As with the aforementioned partnerships, the goal is to help learners, businesses, industry groups, and community organizations benefit from community and workplace-based learning opportunities. Representatives from a wide variety of businesses, human service organizations, educational institutions, government, environmental, and animal care services actively participate in helping Brevard apply classroom-based theory in a variety of settings. These collaborative relationships have benefits for all of the key players, including the adult learner, the college, the employer and the community.

Each key player is challenged to contribute to the healthy growth and development of the other key players. Employers benefit by being exposed to the latest theoretical models of practice which in turn can help challenge both the company and its workforce in terms of strategic planning and skill development. The workplace and the community are stimulating and challenging places for ongoing learning, personal, professional and occupational development, and they benefit from having experienced and motivated adult learners participating in the day-to-day affairs of the organization. Interaction with the community and the workplace enables college faculty to gain a more in-depth understanding of emerging needs and trends. Adult learners gain valuable, hands-on opportunities to enrich and apply theoretical knowledge, explore career interests, enhance and document existing skills, and acquire important practical experience in business, industry community service, and government, while building a network of personal and professional contacts.

The School of Professional Studies
Regis University (Denver, Colorado)

(Tom Flint prepared the following profile after his visit on February 8, 2002. For more information, visit http://www.regis.edu/sps.)

Background

Since 1978, the School of Professional Studies (SPS) at Regis University in Denver, Colorado, has offered adults a flexible and innovative learning environment. Each year, some 12,000 adult students enroll in the undergraduate and graduate programs of SPS, the largest of the schools with this Catholic/Jesuit institution. Most adults enroll in SPS to finish interrupted studies, advance in their careers, and change professions; their average age is 37. In 1998, the School of Professional Studies of Regis University was honored for its service to adult learners and to the CAEL mission by becoming a recipient of CAEL's Institutional Service Award.

Outreach

> The institution conducts its outreach to adult learners by overcoming barriers of time, place, and tradition in order to create lifelong access to educational opportunities.

For decades, SPS has advanced the art and practice of focusing on adult learners. The School's mission is to offer adult learners innovative educational opportunities, foster collaborative, personalized education, develop lifelong learners who contribute to their communities, and to be a national leader in adult higher education. In striving to fulfill its mission, SPS has surpassed expectations by offering:

❖ Courses on-site at the workplaces of numerous corporate partners, including Ball, Coors Brewing, Qwest, Swedish Hospital, and USAA, as well as through its own six campus locations through Colorado and a seventh in Las Vegas, Nevada;

❖ Options for online study in most of its degree programs, including the External MBA, one of the first of its kind in graduate education and now one of the largest online programs in the United States;

❖ Multiple delivery systems for instruction, including on-ground, on-line, guided independent study, and accelerated formats of both five and eight weeks' duration (the 5-week format is for undergraduates only). Accelerated formats create four different points of entry within a traditional semester, and students may simultaneously enroll in multiple formats, as suits their personal learning styles and professional schedules;

❖ Individualized degree plans (through guided independent study) that allow students to customize programs in criminal justice, liberal arts, religious studies, occupational health and safety, psychology, and social science;

❖ Generous provision for Prior Learning Assessment, including the ability to earn up to 45 credit hours (the equivalent of 15 university courses) through portfolio assessment. SPS accepts credit toward core and general elective requirements, with up to half of upper division hours required for the major and half of the upper division hours required for the minor in transferring credit;

❖ Connections to educational partners. SPS is an affiliate education provider with Western Governors University, and is one of 24 Jesuit colleges and universities offering courses through the Jesuit Distance Education Network (http://www.ajcunet.edu); and

❖ Advising and instructional delivery at numerous partner sites. In one of its oldest partnerships, SPS has employed a full-time educational advisor at the site of the Coors Brewing Company since 1988, not simply for the recruitment or support of SPS students, but for the support of lifelong learning among Coors employees.

Innovation in higher education is not a blank slate proposition, and SPS operates within real-world institutional constraints. The School relies upon other Regis University operating units for critical functions such as career services, student accounts, financial aid, and a library/learning resource center. Unlimited flexibility in other service units cannot be assumed; for example, when Regis College (the "traditional" campus) closes for seasonal breaks and holidays, the University library reduces its hours—even though some adult learners might wish for extended hours at those very times of year.

Similarly, SPS recognizes that family issues represent the foremost barriers to admission and challenges to retention. Yet, space constraints and extensive regulation effectively bar SPS from establishing on-site day care for students who are parents of young children, and family programming remains a territory largely uncharted at SPS. Adult learners in these circumstances may avail themselves of SPS options for guided independent study or online learning, if they are so inclined.

Life and Career Planning

> The institution addresses adult learners' life and career goals before or at the onset of enrollment in order to assess and align its capacities to help learners reach their goals.

Regis University has only one Career Services office serving both its traditional and adult students. Since the Career Services office does not report to the Dean of the SPS, the School vies with other units within the University for approaches and services that will meet the unique life and career planning needs of SPS students. However, Career Services has become very supportive of the needs of SPS students. For example, counselors travel to learning sites away from the main campus where the traditional students reside, in order to counsel SPS adults. SPS works to insure that office space equipped for privacy, with phones, laptop computer connections, and other professional amenities, is ready for Career Services staff at the remote sites where SPS students are served. In addition, Career Services offers extensive online services.

Services delivered to adults include group workshops on resume building, networking, interview skills, and online workshops on topics such as compensation negotiation. Of course, some adults are less comfortable with group sessions, so Regis also offers individual advising sessions and seminars on topics such as resume writing, interviewing skills, networking skills, and preparing for further education. Recently, Regis has begun to expand its online offerings in this area, including web-based services providing feedback on resume-building. The office also offers such traditional functions as full- and part-time job postings, alumni/alumnae career networking, and on-campus interviewing with recruiters.

Many SPS students are referred to the School by friends or colleagues who are themselves enrollees. About 60 percent of students come to SPS through "word of mouth." Thus, early on, the School is able to gain the trust of adult learners that is necessary to help them reach their goals. Evidence of SPS success is reflected in the fact that approximately 30 percent of SPS graduate students were SPS undergraduates.

Portfolio-based Prior Learning Assessment (PLA) is another avenue for adult learners to identify their career goals and the paths to reach them. Many students enroll in ED202 ("Prior Learning Assessment") early in their academic career at SPS. Like adults elsewhere, those who complete PLA at SPS report that it is a tremendous experience for clarifying and integrating life and career goals.

SPS acknowledges that it cannot be all things to all adult learners. SPS works best for students with some substantial higher education experience, who (for example) wish to complete those final 30 credit hours for a baccalaureate degree. If the School finds that a potential student is not ready to do academic work at the postsecondary level, then the student is referred to one of the many community colleges with which SPS has cultivated partnerships through articulation agreements, in order to further prepare the student for the rigors of academic work.

Financing

> The institution promotes choice using an array of payment options for adult learners to expand equity and financial flexibility.

Four basic payment options are offered to SPS students:

❖ Individualized billing—Adults are billed directly for full payment.
❖ Personalized deferment—An extended payment plan is offered to those students with cash flow problems. By prepaying an amount at the rate of $34 per credit hour, Regis permits students to carry a tuition balance forward, up to the point of 55 days following completion

of the academic period. This enables those adults with reimbursement plans to avoid having to find other transitional money while awaiting their sponsors' funds.

❖ Sponsored billing—Because of its numerous partnerships with organizations and corporations, Regis simplifies the financial aspect of its education by billing third-party payees directly. In many cases, this means that employers are billed directly for amounts that will be funded from the tuition benefit accounts of individual employees. To date, the School has negotiated more than 230 such arrangements with its partners.

❖ Financial aid deferment—Recognizing that government sponsored awards take time to prepare, students may have the fundable portion of the tuition balances deferred until award disbursements are made. This is crucial to the unusual configurations that result from the unique five-week and eight-week accelerated courses occurring simultaneously within the Regis semester.

Payment methods available include checks, money orders, and major credit cards. Students may phone in payments using credit cards.

The School is proof of the notion that large adult learner programs do not require that the University use "price discounts" to entice individual enrollments. Regis University has no grants or scholarships for adults that are paid with institutional funds (although it does have various awards funded by outside contributions and donations). As a fully eligible institution, Regis University participates in federal and state student financial aid programs that are both need-sensitive and need-blind, and many SPS students use those programs. Moreover, because of its strong distance learning programs and alternative delivery systems, Regis University is participating in the United States Department of Education Demonstration Program, along with fifteen other institutions of higher education, in a pilot project exploring new methods of teaching and their impact on financial aid policies.

Recognizing the scale of potential adult enrollments from some of its largest strategic partners, the School can arrange for discounted tuition when the partner agrees to sponsored billing.

Assessment of Learning Outcomes

> The institution defines and assesses the knowledge, skills, and competencies acquired by adult learners both from the curriculum and from life/work experience in order to assign credit and confer degrees with rigor.

Regis University has defined essential learning outcomes, common for both traditional and adult student divisions. The high-level learning outcomes for the Regis curriculum are in keeping with the values of the liberal arts tradition. They include: leadership in service to others, ethical inquiry and reflection, development of the whole person, comprehensive understanding of truth, lifelong learning, spirituality and religion, concern for social justice, and global awareness.

Both adult learners and their sponsors (employers) have a stake in the assessment of learning outcomes. Learners provide end-of-course evaluations, and employer satisfaction with graduates' preparation for the workplace is a critical component of periodic Academic Unit Reviews for each academic program.

Mentioned earlier was the School's strong Prior Learning Assessment program. Recognition of previous learning is so greatly respected at SPS that incoming students are required only to earn their final 30 credit hours at SPS. Besides filling the gap with potential experiential learning or examination credits, adults may earn credit for military education using recommendations from the ACE Guide for Educational Experiences in the Armed Forces. Credit is also awarded upon recommendation of the ACE National Guide for evaluated courses in business and industry training programs. Areas for earning PLA credit include business, communication, computer science, education, arts, physical education, social sciences, and occupational specialties.

The SPS commitment to quality and rigor in the assessment of learning outcomes is demonstrated by its decision to establish the Center for the Study of Accelerated Learning in December 2000. Under the direction of Dr. Raymond Wlodkowski, a staff of four conducts ongoing research to assess the academic quality of accelerated courses, the value of accelerated courses to students, and the effects of time in class and length of course on student learning and attitudes. The Center's goals are to link these research findings to recommendations for improving instruction, academic programs, and professional development, and to contribute locally and globally to the knowledge base for adult learning in general and to accelerated learning in particular.

Authentic cases are used to evaluate students' abilities in applying critical thinking, knowledge base retention, and applications of learning. Teams of faculty experts from the professional disciplines that their courses represent (such as business managers for courses in management, certified accountants for courses in finance, and lawyers for courses in business law) assess the solutions to these real-life problem situations.

Teaching-Learning Process

> The institution's faculty uses multiple methods of instruction (including experiential
> and problem-based methods) for adult learners in order to connect curricular con-
> cepts to useful knowledge and skills.

The School is renowned for its careful induction of new faculty into adult-centered modes of instruction. Whether full-time or part-time, new faculty members are assessed and oriented to adult learning theory and effective instructional techniques. Case studies, simulations, demonstrations, and service learning are embedded in the curriculum, and guided independent study is often experiential. Since ongoing assessment is a byword for continuous learning, faculty members are trained to observe and assess the performance of adults as key to the learning enterprise. The commitment to the diverse needs of adult students is first recognized through the options available for on-ground, online, and guided independent study. Fidelity to the value of experiential learning is maintained right up to the final stages of degree programs, where adults complete their own 'capstone' project worth three credit hours (one course) related to career or life tasks or problems.

One might be inclined to assume that service learning is the province of the young; but SPS finds otherwise. In 2000, SPS inaugurated a service learning department for adult students. Students may perform service to the community in the context of their Regis courses through direct service, advocacy, consciousness raising, and community based research. Service projects have even included immersion experiences in other cultures, notably Guatemala and El Salvador. To be successful, service projects must be integral to (not an appendage to) courses. Accordingly, SPS has a full-time Service Learning Coordinator to assist faculty and students with handling the curricular and practical issues of this area, both for undergraduates and graduates.

SPS recognizes the promise and limitations of the learning delivered in its non-credit offerings through Corporate Education Services. This learning is highly experiential and problem based, and directly concerned with individual skill acquisition and competency for workplace demands. Although some non-credit instruction may have relatively little theoretical content, it nonetheless can be a pathway for adults into degree programs. Accordingly, when designing offerings in response to client requests, SPS looks for ways to make its instruction not only job relevant but also degree applicable. For example, SPS has designed a certificate in business leadership for its partner Coors that carries 18 semester hours of undergraduate credit applicable toward a degree. In fact, SPS now has approximately a dozen undergraduate certificates in areas such as high performance management and leadership.

Student Support Systems

> The institution assists adult learners using comprehensive academic and student support systems in order to enhance students' capacities to become self-directed, lifelong learners.

SPS is able to deliver directly a variety of student supports to adult learners. This autonomy makes it easier for SPS to create flexible and responsive systems that adults need. For example, the School has its own admissions office and handles tuition payments (though not billing) directly. Students have a personal faculty advisor who works with them throughout their Regis experience. Advisors travel to multiple campuses for the convenience of students, and distance learning students can receive advising by telephone, fax, and e-mail. A Student Representative process provides direct and immediate feedback to SPS, aimed at communication and improvement of service delivery.

A good example of the administrative flexibility of Regis is its handling of unavoidable withdrawals early in the academic period. Students facing circumstances beyond their control (job shift changes, unexpected and prolonged travel, etc.) that cause their withdrawal are given an "administrative drop," which effectively frees them of financial obligations for that term, even though Regis would be within its rights to charge partial tuition.

The School is equally concerned with creating access to educational opportunity for students with disabilities. Components of the Disability Services office at Regis University include:

- ❖ Sign language interpretation;
- ❖ Extended test-taking time policy;
- ❖ Maps on campus showing wheelchair-accessible routes, and utilities/facilities for wheelchair students;
- ❖ FM listening systems, TDDs (telecommunications device for the deaf); and
- ❖ Accessible computer stations with voice recognition, screen reading, and magnification software.

Technology

> The institution uses information technology to provide relevant and timely information and to enhance the learning experience.

The School has found that the best way to communicate with adults is through e-mail. SPS has gone to great lengths to obtain e-mail addresses for nearly every adult student, knowing that if messages are kept short, they will be read and responded to.

It is very important to have current technologies and equipment for use by adult learners. Few adults willingly choose to work or to enroll within organizations that have personal computer equipment inferior to that which they have in their own homes; this is equated with career retrogression, not career advancement. SPS upgrades its information technology equipment every three years.

Not all of the investment in technology must be a direct expense to Regis University. For example, as a result of its strategic partnership with Sun Microsystems, SPS has the use of two microcomputer labs at selected campuses that Sun established for its in-house training office. The labs are used by Sun trainers during the day and by SPS students in the evening.

Online delivery of educational programs and student support systems is an important option available to SPS students. Online, accelerated-format offerings exist in accounting, business, communication, computer science, computer networking, economics, English, history, math, psychology, religious studies, External Master of Business Administration, Master of Science in Management, Master of Science in Computer Information Technology, and Master of Nonprofit Management. Course modules and syllabi are available online for all students. Online library resources include access to reference librarians, CARL (Colorado Alliance of Research Libraries), Prospector (a unified catalog that includes Regis Libraries' holdings as well as those of 13 other Colorado Libraries), article indexes, and full text resources, such as ABI Inform and Academic Universe. Other resources and support services are available online, such as the University ministry, disability services, directory, bookstore, career services, writing development services, and other workshops. Regis is currently building online access to academic records and files.

Strategic Partnerships

> The institution engages in strategic relationships, partnerships, and collaborations with employers and other organizations in order to develop and improve educational opportunities for adult learners.

SPS marketing professionals know that adult students are influenced by considerations of convenience and quality. That is why the many delivery options that SPS offers speak to convenience. What speaks to quality for adult learners is being in a community and supporting a community, whether that community is defined by geography or by professional practice. SPS students seek increased influence and upward mobility in such communities as signs of having achieved their goals.

Traditional colleges and universities commonly recruit young students by having admissions office representatives visit "feeder" high schools. Adult-serving institutions like SPS recognize that employers, labor unions, and related organizations are "feeders," too. SPS employs four full-time Educational Account Executives whose job mission is to visit and build relationships with corporations and organizations that promote the values of education within their cultures, and that have tuition assistance benefits to aid their workers and members.

The fruit of the work by the Educational Account Executives and SPS executives is plentiful:

- ❖ The School works with partners to customize curricula and deliver it on-site. Examples include the e-security certificate at Peterson Air Force Base, the certificate programs at Swedish Hospital, preferred tuition arrangements with Ball Aerospace and Electronic Data Systems, and curricula partnerships with Sun Microsystems and Westnet;
- ❖ SPS partners with the Work Force Development Project for the Colorado Department of Labor and Employment to provide educational opportunities to laid-off workers in the State of Colorado, and with the National Guard to provide educational opportunities to reservists;
- ❖ Regis University is a preferred website educational link for Lockheed Martin and Ball Aerospace;
- ❖ Regis is a partner with Bisk Publishing Company of Tampa, Florida, in the Electronic MBA;
- ❖ SPS Teacher Education has partnered with a number of school districts—ranging from public to private, urban to rural—for teacher education and practicum; and
- ❖ Through its Corporate Education Services office, SPS has training affiliations with the National Association of Church Business Administrators, the Society for Human Resource Development, American Society for Quality, Rocky Mountain Direct Marketing Association, and CCTI (a leading provider of Information Technology Training).

At SPS, partnerships proceed on the basis of mutual respect. Not only does SPS utilize its university-based authority to award credit hours in conjunction with specialized certificate programs it delivers, but it co-brands the certificates with its partners. For example, certificates offered to the Rocky Mountain Direct Marketing Association and to the Society for Human Resource Management are co-branded with those associations.

References

Flint, Thomas A. & Associates. (1999) *Best Practices in Adult Learning: A CAEL/APQC Benchmarking Study.* Chicago, IL: Council for Adult and Experiential Learning.

Wlodkowski, Raymond J.; Mauldin, Jennifer E; and Gahn, Sandra W. (2001). *Learning in the Fast Lane: Adult Learners' Persistence and Success in Accelerated College Programs.* (New Agenda Series, Volume 4, Number 1). Indianapolis, IN: Lumina Foundation for Education.

Chapter 14

Epilogue

This book introduces an informal self-evaluation process by which to assess the Adult Learning Focused Institution. If you have completed the worksheets herein, you are likely well on your way to finding ways to improve your institution's services to adult learners. While it is beyond the scope of this workbook to also be a handbook for implementing your institution's strategies and plans, we do offer a few tools that may be helpful in that effort.

The Guidelines for Developing an Adult Learning Focused Institution Implementation Strategy and the completed sample ALFI Strategic Planning Implementation Worksheet (**Appendix E**) have been created to help you to begin thinking about developing an implementation strategy. There may be other approaches/models that have worked successfully for you in the past. We urge you to consider using them if you believe that they will help you accomplish your implementation goals. The forms in the Appendices include blank templates. Feel free to reorganize these worksheets to better suit the unique culture and circumstances of your institution and the community.

The hypothesized seminars described in completed, sample form within Appendix E can be regarded as part of the initial stages of important institutional and community activities in the pre-implementation phase. Such proposed seminars are intended to assist you with:

1. Informing key areas across the institution and in the community of the aims, objectives, and outcomes of the ALFI study, the eight key Principles of Effectiveness, and the Informal Institutional Self-Assessment Process;

2. Identifying potential sources of support and any obstacles or challenges to the ALFI implementation process; and

3. Deciding whether or not to proceed with an ALFI implementation process at your institution.

CAEL is very interested in knowing more about your successes and challenges in serving adult learners in higher education—especially the outcomes of implementing institutional changes as a result of using this workbook. We thank the sixteen institutions that have permitted us to tell a part of their story in this workbook. Those institutions include:

❖ Baldwin-Wallace College (OH)
❖ Brevard Community College (FL)
❖ Central Michigan University (MI)
❖ College of New Rochelle—School of New Resources (NY)
❖ DePaul University—School for New Learning (IL)
❖ First Nations Technical Institute (ON)
❖ Governors State University (IL)
❖ Marylhurst University (OR)

- ❖ National-Louis University (IL)
- ❖ Regis University (CO)
- ❖ Rio Salado College (AZ)
- ❖ Robert Morris College (IL)
- ❖ Sinclair Community College (OH)
- ❖ SUNY Empire State (NY)
- ❖ Syracuse University (NY)
- ❖ University of Maryland University College (MD)

Perhaps your institution belongs on this list. Tell us your story!

The ALFI Project
CAEL
http://www.CAEL.org

The Principles of Effectiveness for Serving Adult Learners in Higher Education

Table 1.1 Categories and Principles

Outreach	The institution conducts its outreach to adult learners by overcoming barriers of time, place, and tradition in order to create lifelong access to educational opportunities.
Life and Career Planning	The institution addresses adult learners' life and career goals before or at the onset of enrollment in order to assess and align its capacities to help learners reach their goals.
Financing	The institution promotes choice using an array of payment options for adult learners in order to expand equity and financial flexibility.
Assessment of Learning Outcomes	The institution defines and assesses the knowledge, skills, and competencies acquired by adult learners both from the curriculum and from life/work experience in order to assign credit and confer degrees with rigor.
Teaching-Learning Process	The institution's faculty uses multiple methods of instruction (including experiential and problem-based methods) for adult learners in order to connect curricular concepts to useful knowledge and skills.
Student Support Systems	The institution assists adult learners using comprehensive academic and student support systems in order to enhance students' capacities to become self-directed, lifelong learners.
Technology	The institution uses information technology to provide relevant and timely information and to enhance the learning experience.
Strategic Partnerships	The institution engages in strategic relationships, partnerships, and collaborations with employers and other organizations in order to develop and improve educational opportunities for adult learners.

Page References to the CAEL Benchmarking Study

The following table shows the pages in the CAEL book, titled *Best Practices in Adult Learning: A CAEL/APQC Benchmarking Study* (1999), where descriptions of some of the best practices cited in this workbook and used by CAEL in its Adult Learning Focused Institution (ALFI) project may be found. Certain best practices emerged during CAEL's validation of the benchmarking study findings with focus groups of representatives from business and industry, unions, the policy arena, and adult students themselves. To obtain the book, contact CAEL: http://www.CAEL.org.

The Outreach Principle: The institution conducts its outreach to adult learners by overcoming barriers in time, place, and tradition in order to create lifelong access to educational opportunities.

Best Practices Related to Outreach	Page References in *Best Practices in Adult Learning*
Workplace-based recruiting and student support activities.	54, 85, 94
Modularized curricula or 'block' scheduling of courses.	24, 38, 72, 81, 82
Multiple entry/re-entry points for programs.	34
Off-campus or distributed instructional sites/opportunities.	19, 33, 38, 49, 81, 82, 83, 85, 86, 93, 94
'Off hours' (non-daytime) instructional capability.	78, 79, 81, 83
Honoring the language and values of the workplace and/or groups served.	No specific citation.
Flexible, seminar-style seating in classrooms.	No specific citation.

The Life & Career Planning Principle: The institution addresses adult learners' life and career goals before or at the outset of enrollment in order to assess and align its capacities to help learners reach their goals.

Best Practices Related to Life and Career Planning	Page References in *Best Practices in Adult Learning*
Course offerings in Life or Educational Planning, or Career Development.	59, 60, 61, 66
Regular check-ins and interventions throughout the adult students' academic work.	59, 60, 64, 65
Customized orientation sessions for adult students.	32
Re-entry advising on issues of skill levels, time management, and multiple life roles.	21, 56, 63, 84, 87, 88, 89
Portfolio development course for credit.	60, 61, 62, 63, 65
Options for obtaining credit for corporate or military educational courses.	20, 59, 60
Course placement processes guided by assessment.	54, 55, 60, 61, 65
Referrals to networks of providers for services outside the institution's scope or mission.	87, 88, 89

The Financing Principle: The institution promotes choice using an array of payment options for adult learners in order to expand equity and financial flexibility.

Best Practices Related to Financing	Page References in *Best Practices in Adult Learning*
Pro-rata system for tuition charges and tuition refunds.	No specific citation.
Deferred payment for students obtaining tuition reimbursement after course completion.	97, 98
Institution-funded financial aid awards (including grant aid) for part-time students.	98, 99
Equitable allocation of donated or government-funded aid to adult learners.	98, 99
'Off hours' (non-daytime) financial advising and transaction processing.	67, 89

The Assessment of Learning Outcomes Principle: The institution defines and assesses the knowledge, skills, and competencies acquired by adult learners both from the curriculum and from life/work experience in order to assign credit and confer degrees with rigor.

Best Practices Related to Assessment of Learning Outcomes	Page References in *Best Practices in Adult Learning*
Individualized assessment of experiential learning (portfolio PLA & related methods).	20, 23, 25, 29, 59, 60, 63, 65
Student self-assessments integrated into institutional assessments of student learning.	59, 61, 64
Competency-based curricula structure.	24, 32, 63, 73, 82
Multiple techniques used to assess student learning.	58, 63
Faculty training for multiple assessment techniques.	22, 68, 93
Curricula that integrate work- or industry-based skills and standards.	24, 26, 33, 62, 72, 74, 75, 78, 82, 83, 85

The Teaching/Learning Process Principle: The institution's faculty use multiple methods of instruction (including experiential and problem-based methods) for adult learners in order to connect curricular concepts to useful knowledge and skills.

Best Practices Related to Teaching/Learning Process	Page References in *Best Practices in Adult Learning*
Student-led learning opportunities.	51, 52, 77, 82, 83, 85
Course-level structures having experiential learning for credit (such as cooperative education, field study semesters, internships, or externships).	24, 62, 73, 75, 77, 82, 85
Course-embedded experiential learning (such as problem-based, activity-based, collaborative and/or service learning).	24, 26, 32, 68, 71, 72, 75
Individualized or interdisciplinary degree program options.	20, 26, 35, 76, 77, 78
Student-organized courses or seminars for credit.	77, 83, 85
Faculty training upon adult learning theory and diverse learning style.	22, 31, 68, 69, 73, 93
Narrative academic transcripts.	29, 73, 81
Guest lecturing by practitioners.	No specific citation.

The Student Support Systems Principle: The institution assists adult learners using comprehensive academic and student support systems in order to enhance students' capacities to become self-directed, lifelong learners.

Best Practices Related to Student Support Systems	Page References in *Best Practices in Adult Learning*
Intact student cohort groups or peer groups for program advancement/completion.	82, 88
Formal mentoring system using community-based professionals.	20, 32
Remediation or college preparatory programs (refreshers for rusty academic skills).	41, 56, 60
Adult-centered services for students with adult responsibilities (dependents, etc).	25, 64, 65, 88, 89
'Off hours' (non-daytime) student services options.	36, 64, 65, 87, 88
Call centers for student support systems.	36, 87, 88

The Technology Principle: The institution uses information technology to provide relevant and timely information and to enhance the learning process.

Best Practices Related to Technology	Page References in *Best Practices in Adult Learning*
Faculty training programs or professional development funds for faculty for technology-supported instruction.	68, 80, 93, 94, 95
On-line library services (bibliographic and source materials).	80, 88, 95
Electronic information services (financial aid, admission, etc).	22, 29, 80, 87, 88, 93, 95
Institution-originated telephonic student contacts.	40, 64, 65, 74, 88, 95, 96
Student, faculty, and administrator networking via e-mail.	34, 49, 64, 65, 74, 88, 95

The Strategic Partnerships Principle: The institution engages in strategic relationships, partnerships, and collaborations with employers and other organizations in order to develop and improve educational opportunities for adult learners.

Best Practices Related to Strategic Partnerships	Page References in *Best Practices in Adult Learning*
Dedicated institutional staff doing employer outreach.	79, 85
Adjunct faculty appointments from partnering employers and employment sectors.	79, 90, 91
Workplace-based student recruiting, advising, and instruction.	26, 82, 85, 94
Studies of the Return on Investment in Learning (ROI-L) for partnering organizations.	No specific citation.
Assessments of "employability traits" of individual workers at partnering organizations.	46
Employability or "workplace readiness" guarantee for graduates.	79
Discounted tuition for group enrollments of employees from partnering organizations.	No specific citation.
Partner resources utilized: employers' space, equipment, or trainers/instructors.	26

Slide Show on Adult Learning Focused Institutions

A Powerpoint File is available from CAEL.

Adult Learning Focused Institutions

- "Not since the 1970s has the typical student in post-secondary education been a recent high school graduate enrolled full time in a 4-year college or university, working toward a bachelor's degree." U.S. Department of Education, 1995

The 'ALFI' Project

- 'ALFI' is a project of CAEL (Council for Adult and Experiential Learning), a national non-profit, higher education association founded in 1974.
- CAEL and its ALFI project promote the interests of adult learners worldwide.

CAEL Mission

- CAEL's Mission
  - Advance Lifelong Learning in partnership with educational institutions, employers, labor organizations and government

ALFI Project Origins

- CAEL's 1999 Benchmarking Study of six high-performing, adult-serving colleges and universities
- *Best Practices in Adult Learning,* a CAEL book released in 1999
- Study findings distilled into eight *Principles of Effectiveness*

Foundation Support for ALFI

- Development funding for ALFI came to CAEL from:
  - The Pew Charitable Trusts
  - The Ford Foundation
  - The Lumina Foundation for Education

Adult Learners = Great Students!

- Studies on adults (>25 yrs) show:
  - Strong achievement orientation
  - Active engagement in classes
  - 'Deep' learning orientation
  - 'Reflective' thinking habits
  - Superior time management

What do adult learners want?

- Adult learners want educational delivery systems that are:
  - Flexible
  - Convenient
  - Relevant to their goals
  - Respectful

Envisioning 'ALFI'

- The ALFI *Principles of Effectiveness* encourage a vision of education that is aligned with adult students' needs, proven practices that work for adults, and the movement for greater relevance and accountability from institutions.
- 'Old' & 'New' Views are contrasted ...

A Vision for Adult Learners

	OLD VIEW	NEW VIEW
Education is	Courses	Learning
Based on	'Seat Time'	Experience
Acquired	On Campus	Anywhere
During One's	Youth	Lifetime

More of 'A Vision...'

	OLD VIEW	NEW VIEW
Comprising	Subject Matter	Competencies
Assessed	by Test Scores	Authentically
Marked by	Grades	Ability Levels
Plotted on	'Bell Curves'	Performance Criteria

More of 'A Vision..."

	OLD VIEW	NEW VIEW
Shown in	Credit Hours	Portfolios
Recorded in	Transcripts	Narratives
Gathering	Units	Qualifications
Toward	Degrees	Employability Credentials

The ALFI Agenda

- The ALFI Project creates tools and shares information for *institutional improvement* on behalf of adult learners
- Institutions must have the *leadership*, *resources*, *values* or *culture*, and *motivation* to engage in a process of adaptation and change

ALFI in *Principles*

- Adult Learning Focused Institutions *practice* the *Principles of Effectiveness*
- The *Principles* are ...

ALFI Principle 1

- <u>Outreach</u>:
  - "The institution conducts its outreach to adult learners by overcoming barriers in time, place, and tradition in order to create lifelong access to educational opportunities."

ALFI Principle 2

- <u>Life & Career Planning</u>:
  - "The institution addresses adult learners' life and career goals before or at the onset of enrollment in order to assess and align its capacities to help learners reach their goals."

ALFI Principle 3

- Financing:
  - "The institution promotes choice using an array of payment options for adult learners in order to expand equity and financial flexibility."

ALFI Principle 4

- Assessment of Learning Outcomes:
  - "The institution defines and assesses the knowledge, skills & competencies acquired by adult learners both from the curriculum and from life / work experience in order to assign credit and confer degrees with rigor."

ALFI Principle 5

- Teaching/Learning Process:
  - "The institution's faculty use multiple methods of instruction (including experiential and problem-based methods) for adult learners in order to connect curricular concepts to useful knowledge and skills."

ALFI Principle 6

- Student Support Systems:
  - "The institution assists adult learners using comprehensive academic and student support systems in order to enhance students' capacities to become self-directed, lifelong learners."

ALFI Principle 7

- Technology:
  - "The institution uses information technology to provide relevant and timely information and to enhance the learning experience."

ALFI Principle 8

- Strategic Partnerships:
  - "The institution engages in strategic relationships, partnerships, and collaborations with employers and other organizations in order to develop and improve educational opportunities for adult learners."

CAEL View of the Principles

- Based on its research and experience, CAEL believes that the *Principles of Effectiveness* are:
  - Integrated: they work together
  - Indivisible: drop any, doesn't work
  - Imperative: not just 'a good idea'

ALFI in Practice

- Here are some Best Practices that exemplify the *Principles of Effectiveness* in Practice ...

Some *Outreach* Practices

- *Outreach* in Action: Examples:
  - Modularized curricula or 'block' scheduling of courses
  - Workplace-based recruiting & employed adult student supports
  - Off-campus & 'off-hours' instructional opportunities

Some *Life/Career Planning* Practices

- *Life/Career Planning* in Action:
  - Prior Learning Assessment helps identify life & career goals
  - Advising on managing time and multiple life roles
  - Adult student orientation sessions

Some *Financing* Practices

- *Financing* in Action: Examples:
  - Institution-funded grants for part-time and adult learners
  - Deferred balances/payments for tuition reimbursement students
  - 'Off-hours' (non-daytime) advising & transaction processing

Some *Assessment* Practices

- *Assessing Learning Outcomes:*
  - Curricula integrate work- or industry-based skill standards
  - Multiple techniques used to assess learning outcomes
  - Adults' self-assessment part of overall outcomes assessment

Some *Teaching/Learning* Practices

- *Teaching/Learning* in Action:
  - Student-led credit-bearing learning opportunities
  - Individualized & interdisciplinary degree program options
  - Course-embedded experiential learning options

Some *Student Support* Practices

- *Student Support System* in Action:
  - Services for adults with dependents (such as child care)
  - Off-hours (non-daytime) student services office hours or options
  - Intact cohort groupings for peer support & program advancement

Some *Technology* Practices

- *Technology* in Action: Examples:
  - Web-enabled self-service options providing 24/7 data & processes
  - 'Virtual' centers & services that build adult student communities
  - Call centers with institution-originated contacts for adults

Some *Partnerships* Practices

- *Partnerships* in Action: Examples:
  - Dedicated staff Doing Employer Outreach
  - Adjunct Faculty Appointments from Partnering Employers
  - Workplace based Student Recruiting, Advising & Instruction

---

"Fine, But Not Final"

- These ALFI Best Practices are Examples - Not an Exhaustive List!

"How Well Are You Doing?"

- *Your* institution can assess itself - informally - against Best Practices Performance Indicators using the Worksheets from CAEL

For Further Developments …

• The ALFI Project
  www.CAEL.org

ADULT
LEARNING
FOCUSED
INSTITUTION
of Higher Education

Institutional Self-Evaluation Worksheets

To evaluate the extent to which your college or university is implementing practices relating to CAEL's Principles of Effectiveness for Serving Adult Learners, you may wish to complete the informal Institutional Self-Assessment Worksheets that follow. See the directions in Chapters Four through Eleven for instructions on how to complete these worksheets.

OUTREACH PRINCIPLE

The institution conducts its outreach to adult learners by overcoming barriers of time, place, and tradition in order to create lifelong access to educational opportunities.

Legend:
Y = Yes
N = No
UD = Under Development

PERFORMANCE INDICATORS	Y	N	UD	UNIT/PERSON RESPONSIBLE	EVIDENCE
Exemplary practice supporting this Principle occurs when an institution:					
• Uses a variety of special methods and venues to recruit adult learners.					
• Has recruitment and admissions practices and services that address the personal needs and concerns of adults who are unaccustomed to viewing themselves in the 'traditional' role of a student.					
• Works collaboratively with adults to help them overcome barriers that may prevent them from returning to learning.					
• Assists adult learners in making informed decisions about how well the college matches their interests and goals.					
• Hires faculty who perform a variety of roles that include advising, teaching, and facilitating and connecting learners to support services.					

See Glossary in Appendix F for Definitions

LIFE AND CAREER PLANNING PRINCIPLE

The institution addresses adult learners' life and career goals before or at the onset of enrollment in order to assess and align its capacities to help learners reach their goals.

Legend:

Y = Yes
N = No
UD = Under Development

PERFORMANCE INDICATORS	Y	N	UD	UNIT/PERSON RESPONSIBLE	EVIDENCE
Exemplary practice supporting this Principle occurs when an institution:					
• Collaborates with adult learners to develop a systematic process for education and career planning.					
• Helps adult learners determine their level of educational development upon entry.					
• Helps adult learners identify career goals and a plan for reaching those goals.					
• Uses education and career planning as a method of establishing regular contact with adult learners throughout their program.					
• Encourages adults to become active partners in the planning, delivery, and evaluation of their own learning.					
• Demonstrates ways in which adult learners can use both formal and informal assessment as the foundation for making educational decisions.					
• Uses prior learning assessment to help identify life and career goals.					
• Creates pathways for adult learners to gain credit for learning from a variety of sources so that appropriate learning acquired prior to enrollment can be accepted towards institutional credentials and degrees.					

See Glossary in Appendix F for Definitions

FINANCING PRINCIPLE

The institution promotes choice using an array of payment options for adult learners in order to expand equity and financial flexibility.

Legend:

Y = Yes
N = No
UD = Under Development

PERFORMANCE INDICATORS	Y	N	UD	UNIT/PERSON RESPONSIBLE	EVIDENCE
Exemplary practice supporting this Principle occurs when an institution:					
● Provides flexible payment options that fit the individual needs/circumstances of the adult learner.					
● Informs adult learners about convenient payment options.					
● Provides deferred payment options when tuition reimbursement programs do not make funds available until course completion.					
● Identifies financial aid options available for both part-time and returning adult learners.					
● Administers charges to learners incrementally over the duration of a program.					
● Establishes equitable refund policies based on the percentage of course/program completion.					
● Identifies external funding sources that assist adult learners.					
● Has a financial aid policy that allocates awards to the adult student population in proportion to their enrollment.					

See Glossary in Appendix F for Definitions

ASSESSMENT OF LEARNING OUTCOMES PRINCIPLE

The institution defines and assesses the knowledge, skills, and competencies acquired by adult learners both from the curriculum and from life/work experience in order to assign credit and confer degrees with rigor.

Legend:

Y = Yes
N = No
UD = Under Development

PERFORMANCE INDICATORS	Y	N	UD	UNIT/PERSON RESPONSIBLE	EVIDENCE
Exemplary practice supporting this Principle occurs when an institution:					
Encourages adult learners to take an active role in the assessment process.					
Designs educational experiences using learning outcomes.					
Utilizes a variety of valid and reliable assessment techniques to measure learning outcomes.					
Identifies and documents what learners know and can do as a result of their educational experiences.					
Evaluates external instructional programs to ensure relevance and rigor for the purpose of granting credit.					
Advocates for adult learners to gain formal credit for learning achieved via instructional programs delivered by businesses, labor unions, and community-based organizations.					
Communicates actively with stakeholders to identify the knowledge, skills, and abilities they need.					
Integrates the perspectives of a range of stakeholders such as businesses and the community in defining learning outcomes.					

See Glossary in Appendix F for Definitions

TEACHING-LEARNING PROCESS PRINCIPLE

The institution's faculty use multiple methods of instruction (including experiential and problem-based methods) for adult learners in order to connect curricular concepts to useful knowledge and skills.

Legend:

Y = Yes
N = No
UD = Under Development

PERFORMANCE INDICATORS	Y	N	UD	UNIT/PERSON RESPONSIBLE	EVIDENCE
Exemplary practice supporting this Principle occurs when an institution:					
• Utilizes a teaching/learning process that includes a high degree of interaction among learners, faculty, and the community.					
• Recognizes adult learners as co-creators of knowledge.					
• Collaboratively designs learning experiences and projects directly related to the adult learner's work and personal world.					
• Uses multiple methods of instructional delivery to provide access to education.					
• Uses multiple methods of instructional delivery to accommodate various learning styles.					
• Uses assessment as an integral part of the learning process.					
• Uses a variety of assessment tools.					
• Has faculty integrate adults' knowledge, skills, interests, and life-situations into the curriculum.					
• Has faculty members who incorporate the issues, symbols and language of learners, workplaces, and communities.					
• Develops curricula in partnership with businesses, labor unions, and communities.					
• Supports full-time faculty who work collaboratively with adult learners, adjunct faculty and local community resources to develop learning experiences.					
• Provides, or supports financially, professional development for faculty on effective methods for teaching adults.					

See Glossary in Appendix F for Definitions

STUDENT SUPPORT SYSTEMS PRINCIPLE

The institution assists adult learners using comprehensive academic and student support systems in order to enhance students' capacities to become self-directed lifelong learners.

Legend:

Y = Yes
N = No
UD = Under Development

PERFORMANCE INDICATORS	Y	N	UD	UNIT/PERSON RESPONSIBLE	EVIDENCE
Exemplary practice supporting this Principle occurs when an institution:					
• Offers a support system activated by a potential student's initial inquiry about the institution.					
• Helps adults become college-ready by offering academic support or in collaboration with other organizations.					
• Devises flexible time frames for enrollment, registration and program participation.					
• Has faculty and staff who help adult learners connect with academic and support services.					
• Provides support services that address the life circumstances of the adult (e.g. child care, support networks, financing, adult-centered orientation, and advising).					
• Provides, or supports financially, professional development activities related to adult learning theory and application for faculty and staff.					
• Requires that faculty/staff work with the community, employers and/or unions to develop mentoring and advising programs.					
• Works collaboratively with stakeholders to encourage their employees/members to pursue their education and learning needs.					
• Provides support for adult learners at times and places that are congruent with work schedules.					
• Works with stakeholders to establish education extension centers at or near work locations.					

See Glossary in Appendix F for Definitions

TECHNOLOGY PRINCIPLE

The institution uses information technology to provide relevant and timely information and to enhance the learning experience.

Legend:
Y = Yes
N = No
UD = Under Development

PERFORMANCE INDICATORS	Y	N	UD	UNIT/PERSON RESPONSIBLE	EVIDENCE
Exemplary practice supporting this Principle occurs when an institution:					
• Provides technology orientation to all entering adult learners so that technology can be used confidently and competently.					
• Uses technology to build and reinforce community among adult learners.					
• Uses information technology to provide flexible and timely education and administrative services (e.g. web registration systems, call centers).					
• Uses information technology to enable adult learners to assess their own learning needs and their learning process.					
• Uses technology to expand the choices of learning styles/options (e.g. partial and full Internet-based courses, technology-rich on-campus instruction).					
• Employs technology to complement the technology-rich environment in which many adults work.					

See Glossary in Appendix F for Definitions

STRATEGIC PARTNERSHIPS PRINCIPLE

The institution engages in strategic relationships, partnerships, and collaborations with employers and other organizations to develop and improve educational opportunities for adult learners.

Legend:

Y =   **Yes**
N =   **No**
UD = **Under Development**

PERFORMANCE INDICATORS	Y	N	UD	UNIT/PERSON RESPONSIBLE	EVIDENCE
Exemplary practice supporting this Principle occurs when an institution:					
• Promotes use of prior learning assessment to employers and community organizations.					
• Recruits learners through various stakeholder groups (e.g., businesses, unions, and community-based organizations).					
• Collaborates with stakeholders to help establish learning goals that fulfill skill needs and lead to career opportunities.					
• Works with stakeholders to develop mentoring and advising programs.					
• Promotes recognition of learning that comes from training and education programs outside the college or university (ACE, CLEP, DANTES).					
• Collaborates with stakeholders to develop ways to encourage their employees or members to pursue an education.					
• Encourages employers to make a variety of company resources available to employees for education related activities.					
• Works with stakeholders to measure the impact of education programs on their goals.					

See Glossary in Appendix F for Definitions

Implementation Tools

Guidelines for Developing an Implementation Strategy

Stages of the Process

1. **Diagnose your institution's services to adult learners** using the key *Principles of Effectiveness*, Best Practice Performance Indicators, the institutional examples, the informal institutional self-assessment worksheets, and the Force Field Analysis.

2. **Define your goals and objectives** (see next page). What specific changes do you wish to implement upon completion of this activity that will help make your institution more adult learning focused?

3. **Specify necessary resources and strategies.** How do you and your team propose to go about accomplishing your objectives?

4. **Identify evidence of accomplishment.** Specify evidence you and your team will collect to indicate the extent to which you have accomplished your objectives.

5. **Describe how the evidence will be verified.** How will each of your objectives be validated?

6. **Specify the time frames and person(s) responsible.** When will the activity be completed?

7. **Implement** your strategies and monitor progress toward reaching your goals.

SAMPLE OF COMPLETED WORKSHEET

ALFI STRATEGIC PLANNING IMPLEMENTATION WORKSHEET

DATE: _____

NAME: _____

GOAL: DETERMINE INTERNAL AND EXTERNAL SUPPORT FOR IMPLEMENTATION OF ALFI KEY *PRINCIPLES OF EFFECTIVENESS* FOR MY INSTITUTION

OBJECTIVES	RESOURCES AND STRATEGIES	TARGET DATE FOR COMPLETION/ PERSON(S) RESPONSIBLE	EVIDENCE OF ACCOMPLISHMENT OF OBJECTIVES	CRITERIA AND MEANS OF VALIDATING EVIDENCE
1. Create volunteer ALFI Pre-Implementation Team of 6-8 persons comprised of leaders from within the institution and the community.	1. Establish steering committee of at least four key colleagues and members of community to assist with seminar preparation, delivery & evaluation.	September 20 - R. Lopez	Pre-Implementation— Steering Committee Formed with Internal & External Members	Change Leaders Project Team Established—10 people from within the institution and key community members volunteer to become members of team
2. Design, implement and evaluate at least three seminars for key departments, institution-wide, to raise awareness of the outcomes of the ALFI study and seek support for implementation.	2. Prepare seminar materials. 3. Select possible seminar delivery dates and target specific departments. 4. Design seminar delivery schedule, agenda, marketing materials & evaluation forms.	October 1 S.C. Members October 15 S.C. Members October 31 S.C. Members	Seminar materials prepared, marketing strategy identified & implemented	President of Institution pledges her support for initiative. First meeting of Change Leaders Project Team scheduled for January 3
3. Form Change Leaders Project Team to design and develop ALFI implementation plan for my institution with internal and external support.	5. Identify personnel, duties, resources and responsibilities for seminar preparation, delivery & evaluation. 6. Deliver and evaluate seminars. Go/No go	October 31 S.C. Members November 1-30 S.C. Members	Allocation of tasks to steering committee members & others Seminars delivered and evaluated	

IMPLEMENTATION WORKSHEET

ALFI STRATEGIC PLANNING IMPLEMENTATION WORKSHEET

DATE: _____

NAME: _____

GOAL: _____

OBJECTIVES	RESOURCES AND STRATEGIES	TARGET DATE FOR COMPLETION/ PERSON(S) RESPONSIBLE	EVIDENCE OF ACCOMPLISHMENT OF OBJECTIVES	CRITERIA AND MEANS OF VALIDATING EVIDENCE

Glossary

The following terms and phrases are used frequently in this book. This Glossary defines the words as we use them. Remember: Others' use of these terms, or your local usage, may differ from the definitions here.

Adult Learner—generally, a student currently enrolled in higher education who has not transferred directly from full-time enrollment in a secondary school (high school). For statistical purposes, adult students are counted when age 24 years or older. For functional purposes, the adult student is one who has significant life responsibilities beyond that of the student role. These situational and enrollment characteristics of adults may also include:
- Delayed enrollment into post-secondary education;
- Attending part-time;
- Financially independent;
- Working full-time while enrolled;
- Having dependents other than a spouse;
- Being a single parent; or
- Not having a standard high school diploma.

When completing the worksheets, if your institution has a unique definition that is generally aligned with these characteristics, use these instead.

Adult Learning Focused Institution (ALFI)—a project of CAEL that defines high-performance practices and principles for serving adult learners at institutions of higher education. When used to refer to specific institutions, an ALFI is one that practices *all* of the Principles of Effectiveness.

ALFI—see "Adult Learning Focused Institution."

Best Practices Performance Indicators—signs or characteristics that an institution has implemented activities that demonstrate the Principles of Effectiveness (see definition) in action.

CAEL—the Council for Adult and Experiential Learning; http://www.CAEL.org.

CAEL Benchmarking Study—the 1998–99 study of six high-performing, adult-serving colleges and universities, from which resulted the Principles of Effectiveness. The study is fully documented in the CAEL book *Best Practices in Adult Learning: A CAEL/APQC Benchmarking Study*. (Flint & Associates, 1999).

Change Leaders Project Team—a term to denote a group of people whose efforts will be to build their college or university into an Adult Learning Focused Institution.

College—an institution of higher education (postsecondary education) that may offer associate, baccalaureate, and/or graduate level degrees. Note: as used in this book, both "college" and "university" are used interchangeably.

College-Level Learning—Learning that can be equated to that which is necessary for an associate, baccalaureate, or graduate degree from a higher education institution.

Evidence—tangible means of validating a claim about best practices.

Faculty—used in the broadest sense to refer to all those persons whose work includes instructional activity. The term as used here encompasses the following job titles or groups: faculty, professors, instructors, adjuncts, graduate teaching assistants, lecturers and so forth.

Higher Education Institutions—generally, colleges, universities, and similar institutions providing higher education. Specifically, as you complete the worksheets within this book, "institution," may (by your decision) refer interchangeably to a single unit within the college or university—such as one school, college, department or program among the many situated within the institution as a whole.

Instructors—see "Faculty."

NCES—an acronym for the U.S. Department of Education's National Center for Education Statistics, a government agency that conducts education research.

Performance Indicators—See Best Practices Performance Indicators

PLA—See "Prior Learning Assessment."

Principles of Effectiveness for Serving Adults in Higher Education (also known as the 'Principles')—for a descriptive list, see Appendix A.

Prior Learning Assessment (PLA)—a process of granting recognition toward a college or university degree based on the evaluation of learning that does not result from the institution's instruction or curriculum, but rather, from prior non-school experiences.

Professors—see "Faculty."

Student—except as otherwise described in this workbook, learners who are undergraduates; that is, the learner enrolled in higher education for purposes of obtaining a baccalaureate degree or pre-baccalaureate degree/certificate.

Unit—a subcomponent of a "Higher Education Institution;" see definition above.

University—used interchangeably with "college" as defined above.